Gene®

by Carolyn B. Cook

Hobby House Press

Published by Hobby House Press, Inc.
Grantsville, MD 21536

Dedication

Dedicated with love to Ray, Laura, Michael and Tom, and my
chosen family, Annie and Ho.

Acknowledgements

Special thanks to Mel Odom and Joan Greene for their cooperation and encouragement - without them this book could not been written.
Thanks, too, to all of the wonderful people who agreed to be interviewed and who supplied information and photographs: Michael Evert,
Tim Kennedy, Timothy Alberts, Doug James, Laura Meisner, Steve Long, Linda Masterson, Beth Maxwell, Diane Ladley, Frank
Rotundo, Wendy Solomon, Dolly Cipolla, Etta Foran, Steven Mays, Jose Ferrand, Vince Nowell, Christine Curtis, Lynne Day, Benita
Schwartz, Gael Sapiro, Shelley Rinker, Arthur Weston, Isobel Weill, Margo Rana, Marl Davidson, Mary Hennessy, Sonia Rivera, Shirley
Henschel, Shon Le Blanc, and Ann Parsons.

Photographs and Art

Pages 5-32 photographs and art courtesy of Mel Odom. Pages 1, 29, 40 courtesy of Ann Parsons. Original art pages 5, 7, 9, 15 by Mel
Odom. Sketch page 4 and 133 by José Ferrnad. Photographs by Gene Bagnato – pages 10-16, 31, top 32, 33, 34 (two at top left).
Photograph by Laura Meisner/Mel Odom, page 17. Art by John Pirman, page 18. Photograph by Lisa Crosby, page 19. Photograph by
Roberto Brosan, page 22 (left). Photograph by Rebecca Blake, page 22 (right). Art by Mel Odom on page 24 and 25 (top right) originally
appeared in Playboy magazine. Photograph by Steven Mays, page 25. Photographs courtesy Ashton-Drake Galleries: pages 4, 6, 28, 40,
44,5 8-70, 76-80, 87-149. Photographs courtesy Michael Evert, page 32 (middle), 33, 34. Photograph courtesy Tim Kennedy, page 37.
Photograph courtesy Timothy Alberts, page 41. Photograph courtesy Doug James, page 45. Photograph courtesy Laura Meisner, page 49.
Replicas of GenEZine courtesy Stephen Long, pages 53-54. Photographs Dolly Cipolla, pages 71, 72. Photograph courtesy Etta Foran,
page 73. Photograph courtesy José Ferrnad, page 81. Photograph courtesy Christine Curtis, page 83 (left). Photograph courtesy Lynne
Day, page 83 (right).

Cover: "Simply Gene." Photograph by Uldes Saule, Uldes Photography
Title page: Photograph courtesy Ann Parsons.

Additional copies of this book may be purchased at $24.95 (plus postage and handling) from

Hobby House Press, Inc.

1 Corporate Drive
Grantsville, MD 21536
1-800-554-1447
www.hobbyhouse.com
or from your favorite bookstore or dealer.
©1999 Carolyn B. Cook

ISBN: 0-87588-558-6

Table of Contents

"Cognac Evening".

José Ferrand's original sketch for "Cognac Evening." Note the different hat.

Introduction

The *Gene* story is a tale of success that can be told on two different levels. The first is an account of the real-life challenges faced by illustrator Mel Odom when he attempted to turn his fantasy into a doll that would reflect the values and fashions of a past era. The second is a story within a story – how young, beautiful Gene Marshall was discovered by a famous director and became a star of the silver screen from 1941 to 1962.

We collectors can piece together a little more about the story of Gene Marshall with every doll or outfit we acquire. Each comes with a synopsis of the film plot or event in her life explaining when and where she wore that particular outfit. The story of how the *Gene* doll came into being, to become the object of our fantasies and dreams as well as Mel's, has been told in bits and pieces, too, in magazine and newspaper articles. For the first time, though, here is the whole story – the story of *Gene,* and Mel, and Ashton-Drake Galleries. Not to be ignored, either, are the contributions of Mel's artist friends, and, ultimately, the astute collectors and retailers who recognized this phenomenon named *Gene. G*

"**Midnight Romance**".

The Beginnings of Gene, the Doll

The birth pangs of *Gene* began in March of 1991 when Mel Odom drew a face. This was not unusual; after all Mel was a successful illustrator who was known for drawing lovely and exotic faces. However, he had been considering the possibility of developing a fashion doll for some time, and this particular drawing was how he envisioned her in his mind. The face in the drawing instantly took on a life for him, "she immediately became a character. I thought about what would be distinctive about her, that she would be born as a character with a life, and that by adding these little stories to her costumes would give her a linear existence like she could have had in the 1940s."

As a doll

collector himself, he "saw a hole in the market big enough to drive a bus through." Interestingly, too, there was a demand for *Gene* as a doll, even before she was anything more than that original drawing.

After friends of Mel's saw the drawings, they mentioned them to other people who were interested in dolls. Because Mel's drawings of the *Barbie®* doll had been published in various magazines, including *Playboy*, people were curious to see what he would create on his own.

A lady from California called and said, "I'd like to order your doll." Mel's answer was, "well, it's just a drawing right

now, just a head." She asked if he was going to make it into a doll and, coming from a freelance background where "you say yes to everything because maybe only a quarter of them will ever happen," he replied "Oh yes!"

When he started thinking in earnest about creating the doll Mel was drawn to the period of the 1940s, 50s and 60s because it was such a period of tremendous change and development in this country. "I couldn't think of a period I was more sympathetic with than that. Sometimes it's not exactly what it was like, but more how you remember it," he muses.

With that time span *Gene* as an actress could play a wide range of characters. Mel says "I figured *Gene* could play characters from the 1920s if she wanted to, but I wanted to retire her before the whole mod thing happened." He thinks that *Gene* is "a dream of that period, that attitude," that she depicts "how women looked then. She is the reflection of the thousands of films" that exist from that period.

"I thought about the various actresses that I loved and that it would be so much fun to be able to do something intriguing." He knew that the doll would have to have a specific name, but "didn't want it to be a doll of an existing star, because then you have the baggage of their real life that comes along with it. And no matter how wonderful they are, you have to deal with the realities of their lives. So I wanted to create my own icon, that peri-

8

od and that star."

The size for the doll was a critical decision. Mel blew up a profile of the body in all different sizes. "I wanted to create a new scale for the doll, a new size that would make her nice to dress." After he made the first drawing of the doll's body, he had it photocopied in various sizes and laid them out all over his living room floor. He walked around them for a couple of hours, considering that people in small apartments wouldn't want a huge doll and that the tiny ones are difficult to dress. Eventually, just by the process of elimination, he picked up the one that was 15-1/2-inches tall. "I ran around to the designers, who I had been asking to do *Gene*'s clothes, and asked what they thought of a doll just 15-1/2-inches, and they said that it would be wonderful to design clothing that size."

The next step was to find a sculptor. This was accomplished after Mel had been approached to design some miniature mannequins for an exclusive menswear store that was renovating its image. He met with the Pucci mannequin people to discuss the pro-

ject, but the project didn't materialize. However, in thinking about finding a sculptor for his doll, he thought "They've got a team of artists there who do nothing but sculpt the human figure and face. So I called them and asked if they would like to be involved with creating and promoting a doll?" They said that they didn't do that, but one of their sculptors might.

Michael Evert was soon to be a father and was interested in making some extra money, so he and Mel met to discuss the project. Mel brought drawings and photos and Michael brought a list of doll companies he was getting ready to approach because he had always wanted to design a doll. Mel had a 20 minute appeal ready to convince Michael to do the sculpt. He began with "Would you like to design a doll with me?" Mel was slightly taken aback when Michael's instant answer was "yes." Mel was "like, 'No wait, I still have more here I was going to say to convince you." And Michael said "No, I think it's going to be fun. I always wanted to do this." So they arrived at a price although neither one had a clue as to what was involved. What they expected to take a couple of weeks ended up taking "what felt like forever."

"Michael and I worked for approximately three months on the actual sculpting," Mel recalls. He brought in references, and other dolls he liked, to show Michael. "I wanted to start out with the doll itself being really beautiful." During that time, too, Mel met with his designer friends Timothy Alberts, Doug James and Tim Kennedy, and they agreed to do costumes for the doll. "I knew that the guys who would be dressing *Gene* were familiar with dressing real bodies," Mel says, so he was resolute that they should be given the perfect doll body to dress.

"We made her waist tiny, because once you start dressing a doll, that is the area of the body that gets the most fabric – all layers connect at the waist. The top connects to the skirt, and that would be the

point that could look thick if it weren't very tiny to begin with. So even though *Gene* has a very tiny waist, when she is dressed I think she looks very real in her clothes." Also contributing to the choice of giving *Gene* a small waist was the knowledge that in the 1940s and 50s women wore girdles. The movie stars of the period had small waists. Mel wanted *Gene* to be rounded, similar to the Vargas drawings of that period. He even asked

women friends to critique *Gene*'s figure, appealing for them to tell him if they saw something they didn't like. He wanted to be sure that the doll wasn't insulting to women, or that it wasn't so bizarre that women couldn't relate to it.

The first *Gene* was sculpted from Hydrocal, a fine-grained cement, basically plaster, except stronger. Odom emphasizes that "I never sculpted any of *Gene*'s reality. It was all done by Michael's hands. I was hovering over those hands, making him crazy sometimes, I'm sure. But when you turn your dream over to somebody to help you realize it, you trust in them."

The proportions were all important. After the first prototype was sculpted, about September 1991, Mel describes, "we cut her legs in half and gave her more room in her calves and lengthened her from the knees down to make her longer." By making her taller, she became a better mannequin to wear the fashion clothes that were so important to Mel's concept. The first casting of the doll was in October 1991.

The face also changed during the process of converting *Gene* into a three-dimensional form. The face of the first sculpt was actually cut in half and lengthened as well. When Mel is told that *Gene* resembles him, he agrees, "She's got my nose. If my nose hadn't been broken, she'd exactly have my nose, and she has my big eyes."

Tim Alberts was asked to make the original wigs for the Hydrocal prototype. Because the wigs could not be rooted in the plaster, Tim made them to be, in Mel's words "fully ventilated, gorgeous prototype wigs." So the plaster *Gene* had hair. The first wig was blonde, and when it was put on the *Gene* prototype, "she suddenly came to life."

The *Gene* doll is very stylized. Mel expresses it "like 15-year old girls would draw the prettiest girl in the school." He thinks "she is a combination Vargas drawing, Cinderella, Betty Boop, and Jessica Rabbit!" She comes from a number of fantasy places. "Making her seem real to people is important, not making her realistic." As an artist, Mel believes that there is no such thing as realism, "the minute you interpret something, you change it." He explains, "if Lucy (Lucille Ball) had been a real housewife you never would have heard of her. You have to be outside of what you are creating to be successful." He thinks that "the minute that clothes become miniature, they become stylized" anyway.

When Mel speaks of the *Gene* doll being a dream come true, he says "I couldn't have *not* done it, once I thought of it. In fact,

for the first three years, it was all my money that was going into this. My illustration income dropped by half, because I was devoting so much time to creating her. And what money I did have, I was putting into something that is a long shot."

When Mel realized what he wanted to do, he began to worry that someone somewhere else might have a similar idea. "Its got everything: stories, fashion, incredible resources of costumes and color, and character." He thought, "This is so obvious, why hasn't anybody done this?"

Mel considered every possible way to do this project on his own, but he felt "that I was very good in the creative, but would probably fail in the business end of it. If you fail in the business, the creative doesn't matter." Since he didn't have business experience, and because at this point, failure was unthinkable, Mel hired an attorney. It was through that contact that Mel was introduced to his current attorney/agent Al Gottesman, who worked for many years in licensing with Jim Hensen.

A licensing agent, Shirley Henschel, was found by Gottesman to work on finding a partner to produce the doll. Henschel is President of Alaska Momma, Inc., a firm she founded 19 years ago. Her company represents artists, photographers, new product lines, and celebrities. She met with Mel, and "I looked and listened and thought it was genius." Her job in this case was to approach doll manufacturers and to sell the rights to the Gene doll and get it made. "Everything I do ends in a new product line." She and Mel worked together for a year, knowing that they needed to find a company that would not only like the project, but that would be willing to fund it, since there was no question that *Gene* would take money to develop. She says she "stayed with it for a year because it had a right to be made."

Henschel first contacted Ashton-Drake at a collectible show and discussed the *Gene* doll as an appropriate way for them to expand. She and Kate Dwyer (now at Franklin Mint) had numerous phone conversations which resulted in Ashton-Drake being sent six *Gene* prototypes. Mel and Henschel flew to Chicago and Mel presented everything about the concept and all of the details about the character that he had developed. Clearly it had a marketing hook, and everyone felt that it would be a good project.

Finally, a license was drawn up between Mel and Ashton-Drake, a process that took months to negotiate.

Henschel says that "Mel had done everything right. He knew *Gene*'s history, family, and friends. It was a full-fledged project" when he presented it. She recalls that in those days "Mel's appearance would change from day to day." He was always professional, but his clothes and hairstyle would change from one day to the next!

Henschel praises Ashton-Drake. "Sometimes in a licensing agreement, the manufacturer misses the point and (when it fails) the manufacturer blames the concept. The execution of the *Gene* doll conveys things." She explains that Mel definitely wanted a vinyl doll, because he wanted people to be comfortable handling it and dressing it, and he thought that people would be less likely to do that with a porcelain doll. Henschel believes that *Gene* has "been first class all the way. Everybody could see it."

Ashton-Drake was looking for a fashion doll project and liked the *Gene* concept. The *Gene* doll was elegant enough to be able to compete with the Bob Mackie *Barbie®* dolls. (Of the six prototypes, eventually five of the outfits went into the commercially produced line: "Monaco," "Pink Lightning," "Pin Up," "Love's Ghost," and "Blond Lace.")

Soon after, Joan Greene was hired by Ashton-Drake as the project manager for *Gene*. She sold her home in California and moved to Illinois. Mel says that he and Joan didn't meet in person for a couple of months, but that he called her six to ten times a day. "It was so difficult for me to not be there doing it. I'd done everything before," and now it was in the hands of a company half a continent away.

"It was Joan Greene who championed *Gene* at Ashton-Drake Galleries. She believed in the concept of *Gene* from the beginning. Joan talked me through the process of giving up

the final sculpt in order to start the prototyping procedures. I felt as if I was handing over my baby, but have come to understand that Joan's were the best hands that could have reached out. She continues to be my link in the company to make my work the best it can be."

"Joan's versatility and skills make her more than the average product manager," Mel insists. "She always had a vision for *Gene* from how to produce the product to how to best market our girl. I think Joan was the first person at Ashton-Drake to see *Gene* as a complete program, a brand. The *Gene* doll that collectors have come to love owe so much to Joan's talents."

Mel emphasizes, "I liked the people at Ashton-Drake, I thought these were people I could work with, which is a very important aspect in anything this ambitious." *G*

Gene's Biography

Everyone who owns a *Gene* doll is familiar with the story of Gene Marshall. Mel Odom presented her as a specific person and by making her an actress, her costume possibilities are almost unlimited since she can be a different person for each role that she plays.

Mel states that "I wanted to make *Gene* a specific type of person in a specific time period, who would represent not an individual, but a time. Because of my love of that time, I have her retiring at age 39 in 1962, to have an equally wonderful private life as she had a career."

He also says it must be remembered, too, that "it was a very political period with the war going on and people led exemplary lives, whether in reality or just on paper, sacrifice and dedication to the cause" were very important.

Gene's background, as told by Mel Odom, is intriguing. *Gene* Marshall was born on April 17,1923 in Cos Cob, Connecticut, the daughter of Dr. and Mrs. Edward Marshall. From the time she was two years old she attracted attention for her lovely heart-shaped face and vivid blue eyes.

She also was a very fanciful child, given to imagining fairies and other supernatural creatures. Her mother was known to encour-

age this active imagination by hiding pennies under mushrooms in the yard – "gifts of the fairies." Like other imaginative children, she also sometimes thought she saw monsters in her room at night, and her father had to come and reassure her that she was safe.

Gene loved to read, and books heightened her imagination. She was completely mesmerized by the first movie she saw, *Jazz Baby.* From then on, films were her favorite pastime. She was allowed to go to the movies only twice a week, but she prolonged the pleasure by collecting pictures of movie stars and reading fan magazines about her favorites.

Not surprisingly, *Gene* got involved in plays at school, often acting the lead role. When she was only in the third grade, she played the role of Cinderella and stayed in character at home for days. She had the ability to assume a role and believe that she was that character, no matter how fantastic.

Gene's mother loved the movies herself and was very encouraging. *Gene*'s father occasionally worried about his daughter's active fantasy life.

Gene was a good student with a sweet nature. She loved literature and science, but found Home Economics boring. *Gene* was a bit shy, which she covered up by appearing to be detached when a situation made her uncomfortable. She was not interested in boys in her high school class, much to their disappointment.

Gene sensed that her life would be extraordinary. She felt the pull of Manhattan and couldn't wait to grow up and head to those bright lights. After graduation, her parents agreed that she could live in New York City for six months instead of taking the expected tour of Europe as her graduation gift. It was arranged that she stay at the Barbizon Hotel for Women with the daughter of a family friend for a roommate. *Gene* obtained an interview with the Chambers Model Agency and was accepted on the spot as a model.

Two weeks after moving to New York, *Gene* read in the paper about a film premiere. Wanting to be in on the excitement, she applied for a job as usherette at the Regent Theatre. There she worked evenings in her toy soldier uniform and dreamed of the next premiere.

One evening, a famous Hollywood film director, Eric Von Sternberg, attended the world premiere of the movie *Deep Devotion* at the Regent Movie palace. When *Gene* ushered him to his seat he was impressed by her beauty and poise. With great fanfare he offered her a small role as a nightclub flower girl in his upcoming film called *Blonde Lace*. *Gene* was to have only two lines in the role, but she was such a natural on camera, and her beauty so enhanced by the lights, that her star quality was immediately evident.

As her official biography, written by Mel Odom, states: "This was to be *Gene*'s

first kiss by the camera. When next these destined lovers meet, she will already be the star and the camera both her slave and her master for life."

Von Sternberg took on the role as *Gene*'s mentor. When the star Maxine Lester is felled by a "freak accident," rather than shut down production, the film *Blonde Lace* is rewritten to star *Gene*.

Gene fan, former actor, and Hollywood historian Shon Le Blanc explains that the "Studio System" in *Gene*'s time meant that an "overnight success" really had to work hard to achieve recognition. He explains that the studios brought in the best talent they could, not only actors, but writers, choreographers, dancers, designers – anyone whose skills were needed in the film industry. The actresses were trained by putting them into classes for poise, diction, singing, dancing, and so on. Ginger Roger's mother was one of the people who trained the aspiring actresses during that period.

Shon also explains that the studio wardrobes played an important role in creating the actresses' public images. Often someone from wardrobe was provided to select all the clothes for the actress, possibly even what she wore in her private life. The studios often provided the wardrobe for the actresses to wear to public events; many actresses had that written in their contracts.

Once the starlets were dressed and trained, Shon explains, they would be started in a small movie part, then graduate to a bigger part, and eventually would get a juicy role. Often, though, the young stars would be stereotyped; Ginger Rogers in singing and dancing roles, Joan Crawford cast as the shop girl who does good, and so on.

So to the public a star might seem to appear overnight. To the young stars themselves, after going through the grueling training regimen demanded by the studios, the perception was probably different.

Mel adds a few words about *Gene's* story: "People want to believe this story, they want to love this good girl. And want to enjoy her innocence, and her experiences in the sophisticated world of Hollywood. I think

it says a lot about the people who collect *Gene*, that they have this faith and belief in this story. They want a happy ending."

He goes on to add "That kind of optimism is rare in our society now. We're going through some very tough times, and a lot of people's lives are not happening the way they wanted them to."

"*Gene* is something people can have, play with, control, change, and personalize. If they get ten minutes a week of pleasure out of this, I feel I've done my job better than I hoped for." *G*

Mel Odom
The Artist Who Created Gene

When *Gene's* creator was a little boy, he would entertain himself for hours with crayons and paper. Mel Odom has been drawing all his life. "Drawing is where I developed my self identity: through my work, through drawings, through this special thing I could do, " Mel says.

Although he was born in Richmond, Virginia, his mother's hometown, he grew up about 115 miles away in his father's hometown, Ahoskie, North Carolina, a town of about 4,000 people. He was close to his parents, Ethel Hendricks Odom and William Joseph Odom. His brother Robert Wayne was five years older, just enough older to keep them from being close playmates.

His dad was a postman. Mel remembers as a tiny boy being

carried on his father's back in the mail sack. Mel wonders now what people thought of the footprints he left on their letters.

From the first, Mel was an imaginative child. He spent a lot of time watching old movies on television, and he says, "I believed it all!" As a child "I didn't realize movies were a different time. I just thought they were someplace else where people dressed differently and lived in bigger, prettier homes." Mel believed what he saw and wanted to go there.

He was a "Disney Kid" who felt that the Disney animated films were "close to magic." He loved cartoons, and still does, because "they are drawings come to life." His all time favorite film is the classic *Fantasia.* "I think I was like the little kid in the movie

Mel and his mom.

Member of the Wedding with Julie Harris."

"I would draw for hours all by myself," Mel says. He was perfectly happy to be left alone with crayons and "the stacks of paper my mother bought from the office supply." Favorite subjects to draw were mermaids and fairies. One very early drawing he remembers with great clarity was of "a woman making her nightclub debut." He admits that this theatrical woman, probably inspired by some movie he had seen, was pretty much shaped like a triangle. He doubts if adults recognized what the drawing represented since he recalls explaining what it was to his mother, who appeared to remain puzzled even afterward by his choice of a "nightclub debut" for his subject.

When he was seven years old, he began taking art lessons once a week after school from Mrs. Rebecca Askew. He delighted in the art lessons since the small school district in that rural farming area of North Carolina couldn't afford the luxury of

including art in the curriculum. In school he enjoyed decorating bulletin boards and was known by all as "the kid who can draw." He laughingly recalls that one Halloween he decorated a Jack-o-lantern with big red Joan Crawford-style lips – which was copied by all the other kids.

Although a "good kid," Mel was also an active little boy. He didn't spend all his time indoors drawing. He often spent all day playing in the woods, catching turtles or frogs, swinging on vines, or other more common small boy's activities.

One of Mel's earliest memories of dolls dates from his first day at school. He was taken to school by his mom, and remembers seeing a Peter Pan doll. "When I saw it, I kind of relaxed."

From time to time he would inherit toys from several older girl cousins. One favorite toy was a composition doll with bent legs that was almost as big as he was. As a three-year-old, he would drag it down the

20

sidewalk by one leg, an activity that caused the friction to eventually erase its nose. He named the doll "Shaggy" because "that's what her hair looked like." Looking back, Mel thinks that "what I'm doing (creating the *Gene* doll) seems inevitable, but it has taken hindsight and current experience for this to make sense."

He mentions that he realized that dolls meant a great deal to him as a child, but he also remembers being embarrassed and being called a sissy for playing with dolls. Because this was very painful, he says that "here was a degree of a full circle victory to come back to something that had been so much a part of me, and that had been embarrassing at one point. And now I go on national television and talk about dolls – making this a victory of sorts for me."

He attended the Virginia Commonwealth University in Richmond, near his mother's relatives, where he majored in fashion illustration. After graduating, Mel opted for a taste of freedom. Since he was a fan of

Mel's 1959 portrait of the girl in *The Shaggy Dog* movie who "got knocked out and saw stars"!

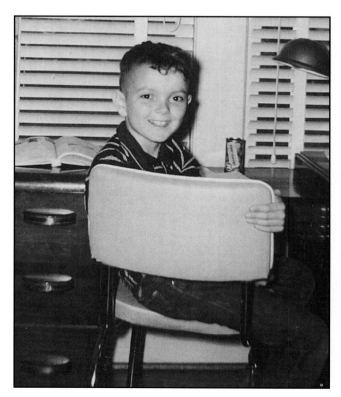

Several examples of
spectacular masks creat-
ed by Mel Odom.

the Beatles growing up, England seemed a
natural choice of location where he could be
independent and be, as he puts it, "something
other than my father's son." He lived in
Leeds, in West Yorkshire, Northern England,
for a year attending the Leeds Polytechnic
Institute of Art and Design, and studied both
art and music in London for about nine
months.

Mel credits an elderly couple who
lived in the flat below him for discovering his
singing abilities. They overheard him singing
while he cleaned house. The possibilities of
his untrained voice were evident to them
since the man was a famous vocal coach. So
for a time, Mel studied music at Wigmore
Hall in London and was coached by his
neighbor. He excelled with show tunes, but

was unable to get an equity card or work per-
mit. So, his English music career ended and
he returned to the states.

A career in illustration was probably
inevitable. Mel had always loved drawing
and since there were no art galleries or muse-
ums in his hometown, his exposure to artwork was mainly from magazines and books.
He was impressed with the perfection shown
in the magazine illustrations of Jell-O, cars,
and ladies. All flaws were omitted, unlike
real life.

Because of his interest in illustration,
on one weekend in New York City Mel contacted an agent, Peggy Keating. They
arranged to meet and he showed her eight of
his drawings. She liked them, so he left them
with her. Several weeks later she called and

RIGHT and BELOW:
Examples of Mel Odom's magazine
illustrations.

offered him a job with the ladies' magazine *Viva.* Since, in Mel's opinion, Manhattan was the only place to have a career in illustration, he was happy to relocate. In 1975 he moved to the city where he lived with an actress and a fashion model. By day he worked on display windows for Lord & Taylor and at night he drew illustrations for his portfolio.

He knew within a week that New York City was where he should be. He came with two books, on Greta Garbo and on Erté. He was in the city for a couple of days when Garbo walked up behind him while he was looking in a Madison Avenue display window. Shortly after, he spotted some Erté lithographs in the window of an art gallery. He went in to investigate and found the artist was there in person making last minute adjust-

ments to his show. Erté gave Mel an invitation to the show and they became friends, and were pen pals for several years. Mel says "I knew I was in the right place when I had access to my two biggest idols in a week's time!"

After the *Viva* magazine commission, Mel began getting regular assignments from other publications. They were "skin magazines to begin with," he claims. Those led to his doing illustrations for *Playboy*, covers for *Omni* and *TIME* magazine. In 1989, he drew a portrait of the Ayatollah Khomeini for TIME. Gradually he climbed to creating book covers and won dozens of awards for his work. He enjoyed making a living from his art. He liked the control it gave, "being able to choose jobs" or reject them. He was given the nickname "Take it or leave it Odom" after he turned down a job illustrating a book for a Nobel Prize winner. His illustrations were cover art for books by authors such as Ruth Rendell, Anne Rice, Craig Nova, Joyce Carol Oats, Edmund White, and others.

What was especially comfortable about the illustration career, Mel says, was "I only had to please one art director" to have his work used. The most difficult part was "that it requires a lot of self-discipline. You work by yourself in a room." But, the good part he laughs, is "you don't have to kiss any butt!"

A time came when Mel got bored with illustration and thought about other directions for his talents and interests. I'd done basically what I wanted to do. I didn't like the notion of getting bored with the creative job. That is

the kiss of death. So, I wanted to come up with something exciting." He considered oil painting and, since he was a doll collector, creating a doll. "Everything that I love – dolls, movies, writing, photography, fashion, and stories – all of them connected in *Gene*."

Mel had become a collector through his drawing. He thought of the *Barbie* doll as a neglected American icon, "that she was the perfect mid-point between Mickey Mouse and Marilyn Monroe." He borrowed a *Barbie*® doll to draw, and one of his *Barbie*® drawings was published in *Playboy*.

That drawing resulted in getting letters from doll collectors and becoming friends with Billy Boy, a *Barbie* doll collector. After publishing Mel's *Barbie* drawings, the art director at *Playboy* began to collect *Barbies* for him. Mel says "I was attracted to the

"Questions" is an illustration by Mel Odom that ran in *Playboy* magazine. Top right, opposite page, is "Sleeping Beauty and the Airplane." Both reproduced by permission from *Playboy*.

detail, the minutiae, not only in the clothes, but the legend around the clothes such as information like 'this one was only made for two years and then discontinued' – that kind of stuff is very seductive." His interest led Mel to attend doll shows and to buy more dolls, particularly more *Barbie*® dolls and Madame Alexander's *Cissy* dolls and "Margaret-face" dolls.

Mel feels that dolls are "very significant objects. Their lives go far beyond their (original) intent." He points to an antique Jumeau fashion doll in his collection and muses about what its eyes have witnessed during the decades it has been loved and cared for by several generations.

He picks up an earlier Queen Anne wooden doll and talks about its power. "This is somebody's legacy. This is all of them that remains, and it is something that is still treasured and admired two centuries later."

He articulates that "dolls walk that line between being objects and personalities, and are both. That is their power – they walk through the fires of time, through plagues, through revolutions, through wars, and remain constant. I look at this doll and she says, 'I exist, I have been here long before you have, and I may be here long after you've gone.' It's a very heavy thing to think about."

Mel's own memories and experiences with dolls have been positive. Once, after he was grown, he mentioned to his mother that the reason he enjoyed creating *Gene* was because he was never made to feel bad playing with dolls when he was little. She said "Oh, honey, I was just so glad you were playing with dolls instead of guns!"

He remembers writing a letter to Mattel when he was a child, asking why they didn't make wigs for the *Barbie*® doll. (This was before the *Fashion Queen Barbie*®.) He received back a lovely reply from Helen Busby who worked at Mattel. Years later, Mel met Ruth Handler, the creator of the *Barbie*® doll, and told her how much that letter had meant to him. Mrs. Handler said "I am just so pleased that this doll mattered in your life." Mel came away excited to have met this woman who "gave me this dream." He thinks that "If it had not been for *Barbie*® doll meaning as much as it did in my early life, I doubt that I would have created *Gene*."

The *Gene* doll is a direct evolution of Mel's drawings. He wanted *Gene* to look like them and to be very much an outgrowth from them, and to be "what I think is beautiful and different." It was important to Mel that *Gene* maintained her difference, "I wanted her to have the same visual integrity as my drawings and to always be identified as mine. There is a distinctive, recognizable style in my drawings that I wanted to extend to *Gene.*"

Deciding to make a doll "was a life decision for me," Mel admits. "I wanted something to give to people that I would want myself." He recognized that it would take time to make a doll like he envisioned. "I knew it was going to be a long haul. I wanted something that had a lot of layers. I drew a face first and thought 'This is my dream doll.

Optimism is something Mel deliberately wanted to build into the Gene persona

If I were to create a doll from scratch, this would be it.' When I drew it in March of 1991, I really thought it would just be a drawing. But I got wonderful feedback from people – even some shop owners called me."

Mel had some experience with doll making, creating the face paint for a commercial doll, and inspired by that, the thought of doing a doll himself had lingered in his mind. The *Gene* project became more and more important to Mel. After he found Michael Everett to sculpt the prototype dolls, *Gene* became more focused.

Mel says the *Gene* project also "saved me." During the time that the *Gene* doll was being developed a close friend of Mel's was in the hospital dying. *Gene* became "the carrot I dangled in front of myself to get through that. I'd go to the hospital – it was relentlessly awful – but I would go, and I would even talk to my friend in the hospital about *Gene*, showing him pictures and such stuff. Sometimes when a person has a very serious and obviously fatal illness, there isn't much to talk about… *Gene* was what we had to talk about."

He believes that his work on *Gene* was a defiance of death. "When my friend Brian was in the hospital dying, *Gene* was a symbol of health, and beauty, and vitality, and it was nothing about illness…It was an optimistic beginning that gave *Gene* a soul. It gave her an emotional reason for existence." This concept was very important to Mel at the time. It got him through that bad period.

"Doing something with a great deal of detail and minutia involved was a way of escape." He says that people don't have to know that to appreciate *Gene*, "but if they want it, I would like for them to know it is there. It was so important to me in creating her."

Mel adds that by sheer coincidence, Michael Evert's studio was three blocks from the hospital. In Manhattan that is a pretty big coincidence! Mel has found that although his original intent was to use *Gene* to get through a bad situation, "just helping this friend of mine somehow comes out in the end product. Other people use it in the same way." He believes that intangible things come out in the final product, whether or not it is obvious or whether they are even intentional." He also believes that one of *Gene's* values is that people use her as their kind of surrogate fantasy. "I treasure the reaction that people have to *Gene*. To me, that is one of its most vital characteristics."

Mel believes strongly that *Gene* should be handled and "played with" by collectors. "I think the whole thing of keeping dolls in a box and not touching them is a drag. It has no real allure for me. I'm no more likely to keep something in a box now than when I was nine years old!" He says the "*Gene* is more valuable because you play with it, make it part of your life. I would rather it have much more of an emotional value than a monetary value. And if it retains its monetary value, if things on the secondary market go up, that's nice. But I never want to replace people's feelings, like 'this is mine and I can do with it what I want to do with it.' That whole 'don't touch it because the minute you open the box, it has lost half its value' thinking seems to me like a real dead end."

People can personalize *Gene*, as far as Mel is concerned. "They repaint her face, they do her hair, they make clothes for her. And even though I might not personally like what they have done, I love it that they feel free to do that."

"I like the fact that people give *Gene* a personality." Mel deliberately presented *Gene* as a specific person, in a specific time period.

M E L   O D O M
I L L U S T R A T I O N

"I think people personalized her from the beginning. One of the things that is so powerful about her is that her clothes are familiar to us already – we've seen them in movies. We've seen our favorite actresses in those clothes. During that period the most sophisticated clothes were worn by the stars."

Mel loves the movies of the 1940s to the 1960s. "I think we were taught some pretty significant modes of conduct by some of these films, even the cynical ones. They had a sense of honor running through them. *Casablanca* is very cynical, very ambiguous, you really don't know anyone's motivations during the film. In fact, they wrote the script as they went along. Ingrid Bergman did not know who she would end up with through the making of the film. But the ambiguity doesn't lessen the moral sense of correctness of it."

He feels that other people love these old movies, too, and like him, "miss that sense of moral certainty of the right thing to do in a situation." Mel thinks that the 1940s was the last decade that clearly delineated that people thought that what they were doing was right. "The country was very united. Films were a way for people to cope…they were patriotic during the war. And then after the war, so many films were made about the bridge between life and death such as *The Ghost and Mrs. Muir.* It was a way of reassuring people that they would see their loved ones again."

To set a doll, "which is already a love object in my mind, in that setting – it just seemed to have a tremendous resonance. The dark background of war would make the vivid colors and the glamorous more meaningful." And inspiration for the clothes could come from the designers of costumes for the stars of that period, like Adrian, who set the fashions for the times. Movies were the pri-

mary source of fashion displays on the screen that people wanted to emulate. He says, too, that *Gene* was a seductive project because he could pick the parts of the movie stars he wanted and combine them into his own creation.

One of the influences that suggested this period to Odom was the *Théatre de la Mode* exhibit. After its original tour of the USA between 1947 and 1951 (the proceeds going to war victims) the exhibit of couture clothing displayed on wire mannequins was stored at Maryhill Museum of Art in Goldendale, Washington. In 1988 it was returned to France to be refurbished and put on tour again.

Mel saw the exhibit several times while it was at the Metropolitan Museum. "The reality of the *Théatre de la Mode* was so moving and the actual clothing so very beautiful, that it was in my mind when I started on *Gene* in 1991. I just instantly placed her there in my mind." The top French designers creat-

Mel Odom and Joan Greene judging a 1998 Young Designers of America competition.

ed the exhibit of couture clothing in miniature in 1944 after the liberation of Paris following four years of Nazi occupation. The war still continued, and the exhibit was a message to the world that in spite of the deprivations and hardships in France, their fashion industry survived. "It was so moving, because originally the things were made in that (miniature) scale because they didn't have enough fabric to do real clothes. They were up against all sorts of obstacles, like the electricity would be on in Paris only in certain areas of town, so they would move their sewing machines around from area to area, or they would keep the sewing machines running by people pedaling bicycles hooked up to generators."

Mel is fascinated with the concept that the French designers were able to create such beauty in the face of such odds. "It is almost like they were creating a ghost in these clothes, white faces, wire bodies as transparent as you can make them." He says that when he saw the exhibit, "I thought, there's a tremendous power here. There is something going on here beyond pretty dresses and wire forms."

Mel envisioned *Gene* to be a character in this era. "The *Théatre de la Mode* represents a very important time for the human spirit – a time of thriving against unbelievable odds. I really carried this around in my mind – and *Gene* would be a part of that." Even subconsciously at the beginning, Mel was thinking about what kind of character his doll would represent. He chose the World War II era "because you had to be brave dur-

A 1991 drawing of *Gene's* profile by Mel Odom.
Courtesy of Ann Parsons.

ing that period, no matter how young and beautiful you were, or even being in Hollywood, you had to be brave." He believes that "what is more wonderful than the human will refusing to give up and insisting on creating something beautiful against the odds of a world war?"

This optimism is something Mel deliberately wanted to build into the *Gene* persona. "The story of *Gene* goes back to Greek mythology, a beautiful innocent selected by fate and the Gods to be special. It's a very old story – it's *Alice in Wonderland* – an innocent in the bizarre environment. The story is such a classic, it is about humanity."

Gene also was intended to have a sweetness about her, perhaps a sadness, since her face is in repose. Because she does not have the big smile of other fashion dolls, people are able to impart to her a range of emotion depending on their own moods.

Mel speaks of the times that people have come up to him and have been seriously moved by the *Gene* doll. "Even with tens of thousands of vinyl *Genes*, there is the intent of where they came from - and I do believe that intent shapes the final creation, sometimes subtly, sometimes not so subtly." He says that "*Gene* has a special meaning for me, but other people find their own content, they connect it with something personal and give it a meaning."

Often people express to Odom how much *Gene* reminds them of a loved one. He explains, "When you hear people place something that you have created in such a personal place in their life, you feel like you have really hit the bone of that individual. You've gone beneath the superficial 'isn't this glamorous or isn't this cute' to something more personal; and ultimately more significant because it carries references that no one else will have." He smiles, but is serious, when he calls *Gene* "a high fashion comfort doll."

Even *Gene*'s name was a deliberate choice, full of meaning. It is the name of several famous movie stars of the period. "Movies at that time had Jean Harlow, Jean Simmons, Gene Tierney, Jean Arthur, Jeannie Craine, and Gene Kelly. I like it – it's a very American sounding name." Also, to add power to the name, in genetics the gene is the most basic unit of a human, so that's why it is spelled "*Gene*" rather than "Jean." It makes her name a symbol for mankind, for humanity. And finally, Mel had a friend named Gene. Odom remarks that "once I thought of that genetic thing, there wasn't any other name. I kept thinking about the word, and 'good genes, genetic, genius' and decided I just had to call her *Gene.*"

Gene's surname was determined when Mel was at home in North Carolina visiting his mother. He was watching an old movie on television and Herbert Marshall's name came up on the credits in a beautiful lettering. "I hadn't thought of a second name for *Gene* until that instant. I looked up and saw the name Marshall and loved it because it had the word 'shall' in it. That was another positive and empowering kind of word. And instantly, that was it. The minute I saw it, I got a chill, and thought 'She's Gene Marshall. Oh, she's real now.' My licensing agent didn't like the name and wanted me to change it to something else. And I said, 'No, I'm sorry, her name is Gene Marshall, there's nothing I can do about it now.' Also, Marshall is a very strong name, because of the marshals in sheriffs and westerns. It's an authority figure."

Mel presented *Gene* as a specific person, and thinks perhaps that is why people "own" her, why they give her a personality. He also gave *Gene* fans what he felt was missing in contemporary dolls – the encouragement to handle her and enjoy her as a doll. "I see layers and levels on which people relate to *Gene*. I think that is my favorite thing about it. It's the personal life she has. You can create a plastic thing and put it in pretty clothes, but to give a doll a life requires something extra."

He feels strongly "that people bring their memories to this doll, they bring their favorite movie stars to this doll — their gestures and the attitudes that they have gleaned from their favorite movie star. I think she has a rich emotional life to people.." He also likes that seeing the doll through other collectors' eyes "is a chance for me to see my creation fresh. Because people do things with it that I wouldn't have thought to do."

Sometimes, Mel admits, he is a little bit in awe of what he created. "Here she is, the doll, that if I saw it in a store, I would have to have it. Hook or crook I would have it. Everything short of shoplifting I would have it! I like that she pushes all of my buttons the same way she does the collectors'. My guiding light has been that I don't want to offer them anything that I don't want."

Asked if he ever knew the *Gene* phenomenon would be this big, Mel answers "Yes. I thought it was going to be huge. Thinking something is going to be successful and seeing it successful are two very different animals. A lot of the time I'm kind of in shock."

Mel's final words on this topic are: "The things you leave behind are children or art. *Gene* is both – my dream child. She is the image I would have fallen in love with on film. I doubt that any commercially made doll has had more of an emotional commitment made to it." This most personal project of his career is also the most commercial, public thing. "I laid my soul open with this doll!" *G*

Michael Evert
The Artist Who Sculpted Gene

The artist that Mel found to do the actual modeling of his dream doll is Michael Evert, a freelance sculptor who is originally from Pittsburgh, Pennsylvania. Michael was trained at the University of Pittsburgh and the Tyler School of Art in Rome, Italy. He had always done a lot of drawing, but after trying modeling during his stay in Italy, he realized that he also enjoyed working in three-dimensions.

Michael's first job was working at Johnston Atelier in New Jersey where he enlarged sculptures using a pantograph.

Artists with public commissions would bring in small models and Evert would help make them up to 20-feet tall. After he moved to New York, he worked as a freelance sculptor doing such jobs as restorations and "ghost sculpting" for well-known artists. His specialty, however, is modeling likenesses of fashion models who sit for him. He made mannequins for Pucci, the company that referred him to Mel.

He had never worked on a doll, but when Mel broached the idea, thought it would be a fun project. He had considered

Mel and Michael confer over the original *Gene* sculpt in 1991 while Mel's best friend Laura Behar looks on.

Michael, in his studio with Mel, working on the first *Gene* sculpt.

sculpting dolls as a possible, and appealing, sideline when he met Mel.

Mel and Michael worked in tandem to create the first "real" *Gene.* Mel came to the studio with many of his drawings of *Gene*, photographs of glamorous movie stars of the right period, pin-up art, and examples of dolls to show Michael the different ways limbs could be jointed. Michael had extensive experience sculpting mannequins, but they were always sculpted in one piece. They would later be cut apart and joints put in so they could be clothed, but they had no need to

Michael Evert with his son, Nick.

move like a doll would, so Evert had no experience in how to joint a figure for natural movement.

After extensive discussion, Michael first made a quick clay sketch, about a half-life size, to get the feel of the project. "It was a way of scaling down," he says, "to have something to look at. It is very rough clay, just a vague image. But it was a helpful step. I didn't want to immediately start doing this walnut size head."

Michael sculpted *Gene* twice. The first was sculpted in water clay and then a plaster waste mold was made from it. The waste mold was then worked on and sanded and a Hydrocal version was then cast from the mold and became the original. Mel shopped that version around and when he found that Ashton-Drake was willing to produce the doll on terms he was comfortable with, he needed a second one to be made 10% larger. Michael re-sculpted the entire doll in an oil-based clay, going through the same steps of plaster waste mold and casting to get an original. Hydrocal is a gypsum cement material that is like plaster, only heavier, harder, and finer.

Mel was around for much of the sculpting. Michael said it was easy to work this way because Mel had such a definite idea about how he wanted *Gene* to look. "It was very clear from the beginning what it was supposed to be like." Also, Mel's ability "to draw to show the shape of the leg in profile" or whatever area they were working on was helpful. The initial sculpt took a couple of months; the most time consuming aspect was getting the industrial finish. After they agreed the head was finished, Mel began painting the features on plaster casts of it. He realized at that point that the distance between the nose and the upper lip was too short. Michael cut the head in half, made a horizontal slice under the nose, and a penny was put between the halves as a spacer. The remaining space between the halves was filled in, making the face longer and correcting the proportions between the nose and mouth.

Michael says that the painting of a head is "what makes the transformation from a plain likeness to an image of a person." He explains that when he sculpts the heads of live models to be used as mannequins, "they are just blank-eyed likenesses in white plaster." It isn't until someone else matches the model's hair, skin and eye coloring and it is painted that it comes to life. The mannequin projects are quick and rather rough compared to sculpting a doll. "The mannequins' forms have to be strong to stand up to a lot of punishment. They are cast in fiberglass, sanded, spray painted, and sanded and painted again. Then the details are hand painted."

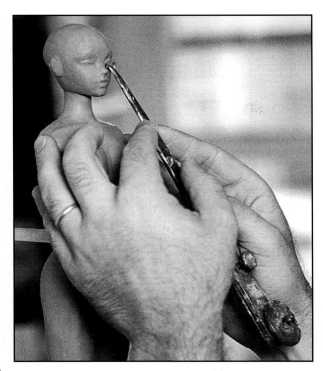

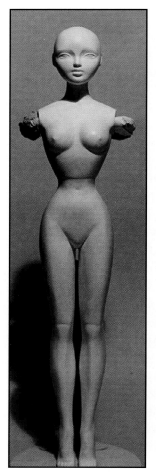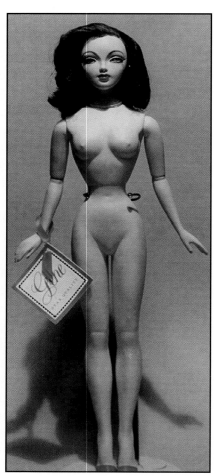

A comparison between an unfinished and a finished proto-type of the *Gene* doll's body.

Michael's quick clay sketch of *Gene*.

A child's portrait in clay by Evert.

"Making the dolls is much more work because, unlike the mannequins, they can't have a scratch left from the sandpaper and they need perfect joints. A lot of attention has to be paid to everything." He explains that "dolls are products that are meant to sell and have to have an agreed upon standard of beauty" compared to his portrait sculpting where "the character of the person is the point, it only has to appeal to me."

Although he enjoys working on dolls – since *Gene* he has also done some work for the Alexander Doll Company – he says because of the technical perfection necessary, "doing it all the time would drive me nuts!" *G*

The 82nd Street Fashion Coalition

Mel Odom's circle of acquaintances includes a group of creative, artistic people who were involved in his *Gene* project from the early days. They were among the first to hear about Mel's dream of creating a new kind of collectible doll. Coincidentally, the three men all live in a small cluster on 82nd Street in New York City. Timothy Alberts lives between Central Park West and Columbus Avenue, Doug James at 82nd and Columbus Avenue, and Tim Kennedy at 82nd closer to Broadway. Mel refers to them as the 82nd Street Fashion Coalition. Laura Meisner, who joined the group later, at that time lived several blocks away.

Mel says, "I can't make doll clothes. But I had friends who could do them better than anybody I knew. I don't see how you can ignore that coincidence!" He says it was like being given a staff, the team was there from the beginning. When Mel asked them if they would consider designing clothes for the *Gene* doll. Tim Alberts' reply was "Yes, I would be glad to," Doug James' answer was "Yes, I'd love to," and Tim Kennedy, who had been making doll clothes for Mel for years, responded with "Absolutely!"

The three contributed their talents in designing outfits and accessories for *Gene* that were not only lovely, but accurately interpreted the fashions and hairstyles of the period in which the *Gene* story is set. They also were tuned into Mel's story line for *Gene*, and their designs express the nuances of the emotions that her roles encompassed. The clothes they designed for her are just as detailed as if made for a person - real clothes, but in miniature – something not often seen in the doll world.

The talents of each complement the two other's – each making a unique contribution. Timothy Alberts' attention to accuracy in recreating historic fashions, Doug James' experience in the construction of theatre costumes and millinery, and Tim Kennedy's ability to translate Mel's wishes into visual reality were a perfect combination of skills.

Doug James, after emphasizing that *Gene* will always be Mel's project, described the gestalt of his designer friends: "A big part of the tremendous chemistry is that we all knew each other so well. It is an incredibly talented team." He thinks they worked well together because "We already had a history with each other. We knew each others' flairs and tastes and could complement them. I don't know any other project that could utilize that."

Mel underscores that "if I hadn't known these people, the creative end of it would have been a lot more scary."

Mel Odom mentions that *Gene* was intended from the beginning to be primarily collected by adults and that adults would understand that the doll "is a fantasy, based on a fantasy." As he expresses it, "she was

"Pin-Up" is one of the first designs that Tim Kennedy created for *Gene*. This is the outfit she was pictured in for her first magazine article, in *Barbie Bazaar.*

never meant to be real, never meant to have the same problems as human flesh. By making her from that period (during and after World War II) I can do fake furs for her, guilt free... If I were doing a contemporary doll I would have issues even with implying fur, but putting it in this time, you are just saying 'it's what people wore.' This is how people looked."

When Mel is asked if the designers were given a great deal of freedom, he answers, "Oh sure, they have to have it. Unless it is something specific I want them to copy." He mentions Tim Kennedy's sketches: "Timmy just makes them (the designs) up on the spot. Some of these sketches took only 45 seconds." He shows sketches of a balloon dress (to be "Gold Sensation"), the original sketch for the "Usherette" costume, and the original sketches for "Promenade" and for "Premiere." He shows sketches of other outfits he would like to happen – a Flower Girl outfit, another showgirl costume, and an ensemble with a red turtle-neck sweater.

As Mel explains, "I've been working on this doll for over seven years, and I haven't run out of ideas or enthusiasm yet!" *G*

Tim Kennedy

The Artist Who Designed "Red Venus" & "Pin-Up"

Tim Kennedy was born in the District of Columbia, the third of nine children. He was raised in the Maryland and Virginia suburbs, and calls Alexandria, VA, home. He says he was "a creative little child in uncreative surroundings" and that "I'm nothing like the rest of my family!"

Even as a child he loved art and art history and was known to walk six miles to the nearest public library to enter the world of books and read about fashion, the history of costume, architecture, and interior design. His taste was heavily influenced by the glamorous world of Hollywood's stylish old movies.

He recalls that when he was in the 5th grade and living on the Maryland side of the D.C. line, his school class went on a field trip to Woodlawn Plantation. He was enthralled with the doll house on display there which George Washington gave as a wedding gift to his adopted daughter Nellie Custis.

The next year his family moved to Virginia, just a mile from Woodlawn. One of the first things Tim did after the move was to walk over to Woodlawn and asked to speak to the curator. Impressed either by the 11-year-old's boldness, or by the miniature samples of furniture he had made, the curator granted the boy's request to make reproductions of the furniture in the Washington doll house. Tim was allowed to take measurements of the miniature antique furnishings and to draw them so that he could make copies. The staff took him under their wing and he remained a constant visitor there, absorbing information about antiques, until he went off to college.

Tim Kennedy met Mel Odom in 1970 at Virginia Commonwealth University in Richmond, VA, and the two have maintained a close friendship through the years. Tim majored in fashion design and had a thorough grounding on every process of manufacturing clothing – classes on pattern drafting, draping, tailoring, and millinery, and so on. He had been designing clothes since he was a child, so all of the production techniques and haute couture techniques taught at VCU gave him a solid foundation for his talents.

At that time VCU boasted an excellent art school and had the number two fashion design department in the country. Mel and Tim were in the same social circle and exposed to the same creative thinkers. Kennedy enjoyed Richmond so much that he lingered there for six more years, primarily working as an ad designer.

Kennedy is a collector by nature, but has never been a doll collector. He thinks it's because "dolls fall into the category of ornamental, not functional, and I live in such close quarters – I like things to be beautiful, but they have to be functional."

One of his oldest collections is of antique sewing tools and accessories. He bought his first sewing box when he was in high school – a Regency box inlaid with mother of pearl – because the tiny compartments were so fascinating. Since then he has collected needlework tools, antique textiles, lace, and embroideries. He also has lots of "stuff" related to work, like buttons, although he doesn't consider himself a button collector. He is also interested in wardrobe-related items like antique jewelry, gloves and ties.

He does admit, though, that by design-

Tim likes garments that are intricate in workmanship, yet simple in appearance

ing doll clothes for *Gene* he is going in a full circle. He made doll clothes as a child, but never thought he would be doing it again. Tim was commissioned by Mel to make doll clothes before *Gene* was ever a gleam in Mel's eye.

Mel owns a Singer store mannequin from the 1940s named "Vera." Mel tells "I bought her in an antique store in Richmond for fifteen dollars. I carried her back and forth to England with me… Timmy would make clothes for it." Once Kennedy even made a gown for Vera out of a piece of Fortuny fabric. Tim tells that once when Mel took Vera with him to London, he had a mini adventure when customs officials took her apart looking for drugs. From their point of view, after all, why else would a grown man be carrying a doll?

Tim helped Mel when he moved to New York City and, through the years, would stay with him when he visited the city. When Tim, still working as an ad designer, was transferred to New York City, he took two other jobs as well – working as a bartender on Broadway at night, and in any free time he had left, developing a business designing clothing for private clients.

Tim and Mel stayed in contact and often Tim would spend evenings in Mel's studio watching him draw. It was a constant creative interchange with the two discussing work and ideas, so Tim was there in the beginning when the *Gene* idea took form. He witnessed Mel's first sketch and went with Mel to talk with the sculptor. When the first prototype was made, Tim made the first garment for her – the "Red Venus" gown.

Kennedy says he loved the original design for "Red Venus," that it was very complex and consequently, very difficult to explain. When it was decided that "Red Venus" would be part of the *Gene* line, Joan Greene came up with a system to color code the pieces so that it could be produced. Tim says "the differences in the mass produced one from the original are subtle." He thinks the silhouette is good. He was trying "to make a memorable garment that would look like it was from a period movie, but not a knock-off of an actual garment."

The original inspiration for "Tango" was when Mel saw a film with Ava Gardner wearing a dress with a neckline he loved. It was, Tim says "a constructional nightmare." But they modified the idea – Tim thought of adding the uneven hemline and the two floating panels at the neck. Tim believes that "a garment should be as interesting in the back as it is in the front." This is especially important for a doll's dress "because the doll is picked up and inspected closely, so every detail is important."

Another of *Gene*'s dresses inspired by a movie star's costume was "Pink Lightning." Mel liked a dress worn by Jane Russell with the bust made in a contrasting color of fabric. Tim drew "a scribble" on the spot of how he visualized such a dress, and the final dress was not changed at all from the original sketch.

Tim says that he and Mel work well together since they have similar backgrounds in the sense that their taste in style and fashion was developed from watching old movies and television. Communication is also easy because they can be direct with each other. "I've envied, admired and respected Mel, not because of his formidable talent, but because of his self discipline – his ability to set a goal and go ahead and attain it."

Tim loves to design for *Gene* because of the fantasy. "The clothing I love to design is for dinosaurs – the women who would wear them don't exist anymore." But with *Gene* "I don't have to consider the useful aspects – *Gene* is the perfect mannequin."

For the first *Gene* convention doll he designed a witch, albeit a very glamorous one. Since the convention needed a "Masquerade" Halloween theme, he thought of a witch in black and burnt orange with a net broom as a fashion accessory. Several changes were made to the original idea – the burnt orange was changed to black, the cut of the skirt was changed, and the net broom was eliminated because it reminded someone of a toilet plunger. However, in the end, it came back in a full circle and the outfit was made exactly as Tim designed it.

The idea from the first was to make *Gene*'s clothes to look like real clothing – to a scale, but with the proportions and detail found in real garments. "Constructing them is what drives me crazy," Tim admits. "The prototype has to be perfect. They are being reproduced in a country where this type of clothing is foreign. They will make a very literal copy of what they are given, so there is no leeway, not even 1/16 of an inch." He has developed some bizarre techniques to produce the clothes for *Gene*. For example, to make a lined sleeve, there is a whole set of problems. To press a sleeve, he irons over a wooden spoon. He uses "implements like chopsticks" to solve problems. But *Gene*'s clothing, he says, "has a quality and look that is not available in other doll's clothes."

Tim Kennedy is inspired by French designers from early in the century like Madaline Vionnet. Vionnet was a designer who is credited with the bias cut so essential to the slinky 1930's dresses. She is also credited with the halter top and the handkerchief hem. She was unusual in that she draped her garments on an artist's mannequin, working "doll size" rather than life size. Tim likes that her garments "are so intricate in workmanship, yet simple in appearance." He has great respect for all the pioneers, Chanel, and any of the Paris designers in the 1950s such as Dior and Schaparelli. *G*

"Monaco" is Timothy Albert's favorite of his designs for *Gene*.

Right:
The plaster prototype of *Gene* wearing Timothy Albert's original "Monaco" gown.

Timothy Alberts
The Artist Who Designed
"Creme de Cassis" & "Monaco"

Timothy Alberts can be called a purist when it comes to historical fashion. His favorite period for clothing is 18th century France, an era encompassing the French Revolution and the Restoration. He loves the way those clothes look with the hairstyles of the period.

He is fascinated that the upper class people of the time were trying to get back to nature and the essence of the simple man – like Marie Antoinette playing at being a simple shepherdess - it was completely artificial. But, he says, "the clothes of the period are exquisitely made. Even everyday objects (used by the wealthy) were pieces of art." The rich women of that period designed their own clothes in that they chose the fabrics, trims and patterns. Timothy feels that these clothes personify the art of France. He

also greatly admires the clothing of the 1860s.

Timothy was born in Flint, Michigan. His father was an executive with General Motors and his mother was a bookkeeper. One of five children, Timothy's early interest in clothing design, he says, made his family wonder if he was "dropped from outer space."

His grandmother taught him to sew although she felt that it was not a proper activity for a boy. As a child he read about period clothes and made his own versions for his sisters' *Barbie®* dolls. He loved period movies and enjoyed history, both of which enriched his understanding of period clothing.

He went to a Community Art School and majored in costume design at Wayne

State University in Detroit. In college he was the undergraduate assistant designer for theatre productions. He designed costumes, draping and sewing them, while also learning stage craft.

The theatre "recreates on stage a period and brings it back to life," he explains. "There is a certain etiquette to wearing clothes of any period, and it is fun to recreate them." The way clothing is constructed affects how people move. He was fortunate while in school to work with a woman who was an extremely skilled couturiere, and who created the gowns for Miss Black America.

His second major was art history. He was exposed to a lot of artwork and was spurred to look further into the history and fashions of the time when the paintings were done. Looking back, he says he would go into museum work if he could start over. An ideal job, Timothy says, would be a curator at a museum caring for clothing and learning restoration techniques.

I try to make miniature clothes, not doll clothes, I make real seams, make a reduction in miniature of real clothes

When he moved to New York City in 1974, Timothy talked with Diana Vreeland about working at the Metropolitan. However, after she told him that "everyone there is on trust funds, no one gets paid" he decided to look further afield.

When Timothy first moved to New York, he expected to design for theatres, so he worked for a series of major costume houses. Finding that group cliquish and clannish, he was disheartened with the real world. However, through a friend he found out that extra people were needed for a Circle in the Square production of *Tartuffe* which led to jobs on Broadway and to joining the union. After designing for the theatre, he moved to working for soap operas on television. Timothy describes that as "boring. I just watched on the set to see that the clothes were perfect." He also did commercials and some film work.

Alberts' primary work is as a costume supervisor. He works with the designers to make certain there are enough duplicate costumes, to watch continuity on the set. The biggest challenge, he thinks, "is getting along with people. I work with the actors and directors" and has to keep everyone satisfied.

The most recent film he worked on, over a three month period, was *At First Sight* with Val Kilmer. Last year, for 13 months off and on, he worked on *The Devil's Own*. In that instance, one of the "perks" was the opportunity to travel to Dublin and Paris.

Alberts was working in a friend's gift shop when Mel Odom came in as a customer. About six years ago, Alberts began attending doll shows with Mel and Doug James.

Mel had often talked with his friends about his idea for creating a doll. And when it came time for the prototype *Gene* to have a wig, Alberts was the perfect person to ask. Timothy had learned to make wigs from one of the best wig makers in the world, Paul Huntley. Originally from England, Huntley creates wigs for films and Broadway shows.

The best wigs were originally made on a lace cap, an open weave net made of human hair. Now the lace or tulle caps are made of cotton silk, and the hair for the wig is knotted into it with a crochet hook.

For *Gene*, Alberts knotted two or three hairs at a time with an extra fine crochet hook. Synthetic hair is best for dolls since real hair tends to knot when working on such a small scale. The most difficult part of making the wigs for *Gene* was to get the lace cap to fit snugly on her tiny head. The hair was styled after it was all attached to the cap. Those lovely styles from the prototype wigs had to be simplified after the rooted hair dolls were made, since that is a totally different situation.

Alberts describes his process of creating fashions for *Gene*: " I'd make the things I wanted to make. Then they would be approved by Mel and he sent them to Ashton-Drake." At that point, the team at Ashton-Drake decided if any changes were to be made. Timothy says that some changes were made to "Night at Versailles," for example. "The original dress was done for the Santa Barbara show with the color an ash of rose lined with dark rose." The color was changed and the coat left off for the mass-produced version.

Much research goes into every outfit designed by Alberts. "I try not to copy somebody else's dress, unless it is intended to be an interpretation of a Dior or another designer. I look through old magazines and let the ideas stew. I make sketches deciding 'how do they make this collar' but try to make the dress original." He might be inspired by a piece of fabric.

For dolls, he says, "the hardest thing is to find the right scale, weight, and surface design" because of their small size. "I try to make miniature clothes, not doll clothes,"

I try not to copy anyone else's dress, unless it is intended as an intrepretation of a Dior or another designer

Alberts explains. "I make real seams, make a reduction in miniature of real clothes." He likes making clothes for dolls, though, because "they don't talk back!" He remembers making wedding dresses for people, not a favorite job. "Brides get a little crazy!"

Alberts designs a dress by draping *Gene* with muslin to achieve the style he envisions. Sometimes he redoes the muslin dress three or four times before he comes up with a finished pattern. He emphasizes that "a 1/16 of an inch deviation can be a big problem" when working on such a small scale.

"Monaco," Albert's favorite of his designs for *Gene,* was originally designed for the plaster prototype doll. The bodice was made from a piece of antique lace and the roses on the skirt were larger. The headpiece had a big bow in the back and was larger since it was based on a Russian court headdress and was meant to fit down on the head. The most difficult to fit of his outfits for *Gene* was "Midnight Romance." The gown "was a horror making," he claims, "because there is so much tulle in the skirt." The original of "Creme de Cassis" was created with antique Victorian lace.

Timothy's genius is apparent in the classic outfits he has created for *Gene*: "Monaco," "Blue Evening," "Striking Gold," "Incognito," "El Morocco," "Midnight Romance," and "Night at Versailles." *G*

Originally, Doug James envisioned "Good-Bye New York" and "Hello Hollywood Hello" as a set.

44

Doug James
The Artist Who Designed
"Good-bye New York"

Trained as an actor, Doug James began his designing career more or less as a fluke. He was an acting intern at the Williamstown Theatre Festival located in Massachusetts. The interns and production people rotated jobs, and he was working a stint in the costume shop. His first show was *Ring Around the Moon* and because no one in the costume shop was experienced, he ended up draping and making a silk chiffon dress for Blythe Danner. His success led to his working in the costume shop all summer and liking it enough to return several more summers.

Doug is originally from several small towns in mid-western Michigan – Doug's father was a Methodist minister and the family would move with each church assignment. James

went to school at East Michigan University and graduated from the University of Michigan with a degree in theatre arts. His training included stagecraft, lighting, and costumes. Doug says, "I was drawn to the costume shops, but was always doing acting or stagecraft." He also did an extended study at the Shakespeare Institute in England. There he would study the text of the plays during the day and see the performances at night.

He then moved to New York City where he had several colorful jobs: sewing mirrors on elephant blankets for a circus, working at the Julliard School as a milliner, and pretending to play a night club piano on the "soap" *Another World*.

In 1986 he left New York for a year and a half, first working as artistic director of

45

a theatre company outside Chicago, and then attempting to put together another theatre company. But when funding fell through, he returned to New York. This time his focus was on costumes rather than acting. He received a call from the *Phantom of the Opera* people who were planning the first tour of the show. He was asked to bid on making the hats for the tour group and even though he didn't have the space, he bid on the job. When he got the assignment, he sublet an extra room intending it to be a workspace for a couple of months. He still is using it as his studio.

After making the hats for the Phantom tour, he was asked to replace the ones in the New York production, then for the California and the Canadian productions. His credits include working on the stage productions of *The Beauty and the Beast, Will Rogers Follies,* and *Candida.* He also was active working for films. He made the hats for Shirley McLaine in *Guarding Tess,* for *Wyatt Erp* with Kevin Costner, for *Sebrina* with Harrison Ford, and *Stranger Among Us* with Melanie Griffith, as well as for the Ballet Hispanico.

Doug James was a milliner for two Muppet's movies and they aided him on Hello Hollywood, Hello ...the staff custom dyed the blue fur for Gene's collar

His favorite film jobs, though, have been the Muppet movies. He was milliner for the *Muppet Christmas Carol* in which he made 180 hats for the puppets, and *Muppet Treasure Island* in which he made hats for the actors like Tim Curry as well as the Muppets. He is full of admiration for Polly Smith who is the costume designer for the Muppets, because "she is more accurate on puppets and better than some designers are on people!"

In television, *Sesame Street* and *The World of Dr. Seuss* have also used his talents. And in 1989/90 he began working for *Saturday Night Live.* He is now Assistant Head of Wardrobe for *SNL,* and friends describe his hectic weekends when the show is in season as his "being in the vortex!"

Doug has known Tim Alberts for 20 years – they met at Julliard – and Mel Odom for a long time. He met Mel through a mutual friend who was a doll collector. They began going to doll shows together.

Doug made soft sculptured dolls for a consignment shop called Ruelles. His first attempt was a doll with a cone-shaped body dressed in a cavalier gown. That was followed by a window full of dolls dressed in similar outfits. Later, James also made a series of seven soft sculpture dolls for an art gallery on the East Side. John Darcy Noble encouraged him to make a Beauty and the Beast doll after seeing a doll of Maria Callas he had made. Both of these, and a Bride doll, were featured in exhibits at the Museum of the City of New York.

Mel had been formulating *Gene* for a long time, and naturally he spoke about it with his friends since he was aware of their clothing backgrounds. Mel asked Doug to do something inspired by the movie *The Ghost and Mrs. Muir.* He took the basic elements and ended up with what became the "Loves Ghost" outfit.

With many of the outfits Doug has designed for *Gene,* the inspiration began with a dress from an old movie. Mel often tapes films with ideas for clothes, which he runs by the designers. For "Crescendo" Mel had spotted a dress that had a neckline he loved. Doug translated the neckline into something suitable for *Gene*, and designed the gown around it. He suggested to Mel that *Gene* should be carrying sheet music if she were going to be a violinist. Mel agreed, but said the score had to be *Humoresque!*

"Afternoon Off" was Doug's idea to contrast with all of the fancy gowns that had been created for *Gene*. The original version was a one-of-a-kind doll that was raffled off at a Gay Men's Health Crisis dancethon. (The GMHC is an AIDS services organization.) Laura Meisner created a Lana Turneresque ponytail hairstyle to be compatible with the casual outfit. The original version had a buff colored jacket with a soft blue plaid skirt, a brown leather purse, wristwatch, and a head scarf of a plum, magenta, and tangerine print. Doug's aim was "to make it look like a real thing, since most of *Gene's* other clothes were so costumy."

"Hello Hollywood, Hello" was a project that Doug almost gave up on – he designed it five times. He had originally visualized that and "Goodbye New York" as a combination gift set, so his original designs were contrasts between the climate, formality/informality of California versus New York City. The Muppets aided him on "Hello Hollywood, Hello" – the designers custom dyed the blue fur for *Gene's* collar.

Doug says, "the factory which makes the *Gene* clothing is very good with precise tailored things." The outfits that are draped and that need an artistic eye are much harder

I make a special point to include a hankerchief or accessory that would be appropriate for the outfit or to the moment Gene is wearing it

in any mass production situation. He thinks they did a good job with "Goodbye New York." That outfit required a lot of research into clothing from the 1941 era. Mel taped a woman entertainer in an old movie who was wearing a costume with fur around the shoulders. Doug saw a Joan Crawford film in which the star wore a tailored suit with a square cut neckline that allowed more color around the face. The original design had a tiny lipstick and Doug had hoped that miniature train tickets and a train schedule could be made to go with it.

The hatbox he designed is just like the prototype. He wanted striped paper on the side, so he cut stripes of colored, textured paper out of magazines and pasted them together for the right look, then photocopied it to cover the hatbox. He is impressed at that fidelity. "One of the neatest things is that something that small is exactly right. We (designers) might as well go to the extra effort to make something like that hatbox, because it might happen" in the final mass-produced version. (The blue logo on the box is a remnant of the original color scheme when the blouse and gloves were blue rather than red.) Doug thinks the little things are very important in the *Gene* outfits. "I make a special point to include a handkerchief or accessory that would be appropriate for the outfit or to the moment *Gene* is wearing it." More detail makes the ensembles much more interesting. He found out in his ten years of decorating the Lord & Taylor Christmas windows that either bold design and garish colors or small detail can attract attention. *G*

"Iced Coffee"
by Laura Meisner.

Laura Meisner

Gene's Hairstylist

Laura Meisner has loved dolls all her life. She knows that as a young child in Puerto Rico she had baby dolls to play with. But her earliest memory is a fleeting glimpse of an *I Dream of Jeannie* doll in a neighbor girl's hand. Enthralled at the doll attired in pink with high-heeled shoes, Laura never saw the child again, but never forgot the doll. Finally just a few years ago, Laura found one of those 20-inch *Jeannie* dolls, dressed in the same pink outfit, for her collection.

Laura turned into an adult doll collector when she bought a "Made in USA" hard plastic doll on a whim. "It was a wreck!" she exclaims. "The face was so sweet. I paid $60. for her, which was highway robbery – that doll should have been in the garbage!" But after taking her home, she bathed the doll, gave it a beautiful hairstyle, bought her clothes, and named it Jennifer. Sadly, Laura says, after a few years, Jennifer developed an odor "so putrid I had to let her go."

But by the time of Jennifer's affliction, Laura was already a passionate collector, having discovered a doll hospital in New

York that sold dolls. She had accumulated *Kisses, Midges, Ellipses, Barbie®* dolls, Revlon dolls, and her favorite, *Jill.* Connected to her doll hobby was her willingness to groom dolls belonging to her friends – among them Mel Odom.

She and Mel met ten years ago. He had placed an ad in *Barbie Bazaar* concerning a doll for sale. Laura had called to inquire about it and had left a message on his answering machine. A few days later, returning from a Farley Dickinson Doll Show on the same bus, since they lived in the same section of Manhattan, Laura made a comment to designer Doug James who was with Mel, and Mel recognized her distinctive voice.

Laura designed many of *Gene's* hair styles. Although she has no formal training in hairdressing, Laura had a lot of practical experience. When her family moved to the United States just before her tenth birthday, they lived only a block away from a beauty salon. The woman who operated the salon befriended Laura, let her watch while she worked on customers, and as time went on taught her how to frost hair, apply makeup, how to do a beehive, and so on. Laura experimented with all of these new techniques with her mother's hair. When Laura was a young teenager, her mother was a testament to Laura's skills – modeling frequently changing hair colors and styles.

From the age of six, when she discovered "ballet" in the *Encyclopedia Britannica*, Laura had been training as a classical ballerina. So applying stage makeup and hair dressing were a part of preparing herself to dance.

She also spent many hours as a child playing with the hair of her younger sister's dolls – *Crissy* and *Velvet*. Even though the grow-hair dolls belonged to her sister, Laura wouldn't let her play with them, but says, "I played with them until they were bald!" Laura's very favorite of the *Crissy* family dolls was *Mia,* "because her name means 'mine' in Spanish."

Laura became involved with *Gene* hairstyling through Timothy Alberts. He had been asked by Mel to create some hand-ventilated wigs for the plaster *Gene* prototypes. Alberts made wonderful miniature wigs for the plaster dolls, but was inexperienced with vinyl dolls with rooted hair, so Laura joined the team.

Some of the hairstyles Laura pioneered for *Gene* are the French twist on "Gold Sensation" and the coiffure on "Pin Up." For each hairstyle, Laura groomed three to five dolls.

With "Blue Goddess" the factory workers seemed unable to duplicate the hairstyle of the prototype dolls. To teach them how the hair was "constructed," Laura and Mel decided to make a video tape to send to them. Mel taped Laura doing the styling, from start to finish showing at what length and how the hair was cut, how it was set, and how to steam it for the finished hairdo. Laura feels that because *Gene* is such a fashion mannequin, her hair really needed finessing and that was difficult to get at the factory. She explains that "unlike a garment there is no pattern for a hairstyle, and when the workers have quotas of so many dolls to finish a day, they don't have time to finesse the hair."

"I think *Gene* is a sexy and sensuous doll," Laura states, "and those qualities inspired me to create hairstyles to complement her appearance. It is very rewarding working with *Gene* – she's such a beautiful doll."

Not only has Laura worked on *Gene*'s hair, but she has also designed two of her ensembles: "Iced Coffee" and "Embassy Luncheon."

Laura learned to sew from her husband Danny's cousin, Charlotte Meisner, now in her late 80s. Laura learned the basics of sewing so that she could duplicate in miniature one of Charlotte's dresses from the early 1900s for a Schoenhut doll that belonged to Doug James. Laura also spent a lot of time in Doug's studio watching him design, and asked him questions. Laura had wanted to design something for *Gene*, so she worked on "Iced Coffee" in Doug's studio.

"Embassy Luncheon" was first seen as a one-of-a-kind at the first *Gene* convention. It was also done in Doug's studio. Laura describes how a dress for *Gene* is designed: "We start out with pins and a piece of muslin and drape the doll. When the draping is what we want, a muslin dress is made. The muslin dress is taken apart and a paper pattern is made from it. If there are defects, a second muslin dress is made. When it fits perfectly, we go to the fashion fabrics. Then," she says, "because silk chiffon is so different from cotton, you cry a lot!" *G*

High Drama

Ashton-Drake Galleries

For a doll to be successful, having a concept and developing a prototype is only the beginning. Mel, as a creative person, easily handled these beginning steps. When it came to the question of producing the doll, promoting it and marketing it, he realized he needed experts in those areas.

The Ashton-Drake Galleries is headquartered in the Chicago area, in Niles, Illinois. Founded in 1985 as part of the Bradford Group of collectible companies, it has grown to become the world's largest direct marketer of limited edition dolls. From the very beginning, Ashton-Drake has produced award-winning dolls, and has been committed to giving value and quality to their customers.

Ashton-Drake's parent company, the Bradford Group, is one of the oldest and largest direct response marketers of collectible products. The company includes the

"When I went to see Ashton-Drake, I had six prototypes made and dressed," Mel recalls. Up until they were involved, Mel says his business plan was "winging it, winging it all."

Bradford Exchange which specializes in plates; Hawthorne Architectural Register, in cottages; Longton Crown, in steins; and Norman Rockwell Galleries, in figurines.

Before *Gene*, the major part of Ashton-Drake's business was in producing high quality, reasonably priced baby and children dolls by such well-known artists as Wendy Lawton, Yolanda Bello, Kathy Barry-Hippensteel, Diana Effner, Cindy McClure, Brigitte Deval, Julie Good-Kruger, and Titus Tomescu. The Ashton-Drake dolls are marketed in Canada, the United Kingdom, Europe and Australia through branch offices, as well as throughout the United States.

The first doll marketed by Ashton-Drake was "Jason," designed by Yolanda Bello. "Jason," a little boy in a clown costume, was originally offered to collectors in

51

1985 and 1986 for $48. The majority of the dolls following were similar cute or funny bisque children. The only lady or fashion dolls they had attempted were bride dolls. So *Gene* was something new and different for them.

Ashton-Drake's traditional method of merchandising dolls was to maintain a fast turnover – a doll would be advertised, sold, and a new one prepared to take its place. But collectors were slow to respond to *Gene* because she was so different from what was known to the general public at the time. It required a more detailed public relations and advertising campaign to get the message of *Gene* across.

Until *Gene* there was very little point of reference for such a fashion doll in the general market. Many collectors who liked fashion dolls were so entrenched with the 11-1/2-inch size dolls that they didn't relate to the taller and more realistic woman's proportions. *Gene* was a cutting edge doll for any company, and as the deadline was coming up to renew Mel's option, things were not looking good for the *Gene* project.
Linda Masterson explains that "at Ashton-Drake, it is survival of the most popular. When dolls don't work they get sent to dolly prison. They don't get parole and they don't get a second chance."

Efforts on Gene's Behalf

Mel and the others who were closely involved with the *Gene* doll felt that the project still needed time, but the concept was strong, and the idea was right, that the problem was that *Gene* was breaking new ground and needed time to find her public.

Mel says that "one thing I've learned from all this is that the human spirit will proceed. There are ways around almost any obstacles. During the period of my developing *Gene* I had so many friends die. And at this worst of times with *Gene*, that wasn't what I was going through. So it put all those problems in perspective. It was, like this is very discouraging, but I'm not dying from this. I'm going on to something else from this." He goes on to explain, "It's that refusal to give in. I just escorted people to the Pearly Gates left and right. *Gene* was sort of my refuge. She was my place to go to, my aspirations and dreams to go on with."

Deciding that with all of the synchronistic good luck that he had enjoyed so far with the *Gene* project that persistence was the only road, Mel and the others involved began calling in favors on *Gene's* behalf.

Laura Meisner and Doug James decided that part of the problem was perception - that people had not seen *Gene's* beautifully sculpted body. Laura arranged to write an article about the new *Gene* doll to be published in *Barbie Bazaar* magazine. She and Doug thought about creating a bathing suit to show off *Gene's* fantastic figure, but Tim Kennedy had already created "Pin Up" and they borrowed that outfit for the photo shoot. Laura styled the doll's hair in a tight controlled hairdo, typical of *Gene's* story period. Then they photographed the doll as flatteringly as possible to illustrate the article. Showing *Gene* in that new light brought immediate response. Suddenly, in just a day or two after the article appeared, the phones began ringing with orders for the new fashion doll.

As early as January 1996 there were articles about *Gene* showing up, but there was little information from Ashton-Drake and people didn't know how to order the doll.

Gene's promotion was helped even earlier by discussions about her on the Internet. As Sonia Rivera, editor of the newsletter *Gene Scene*, says "The basic ground work for *Gene* collectors came about online. That made *Gene* a trend setter and opened up a large new area of collecting." She goes on to explain "the groups online kept close tabs on what was happening and wrote to Ashton-Drake." In an interview by Beauregard Houston-Montgomery in the *Doll Journal*, Mel agrees, "Early on the Internet was very, very good for *Gene* because it was a way of measuring the grass roots support for her. It was very beneficial for us in the beginning…I would send (pages of Internet comments) to Ashton-Drake, because they weren't aware of the interest in *Gene* at that time. I have a very good friend since college, Stephen Long, who started up an online magazine about my doll called *Genezine*."

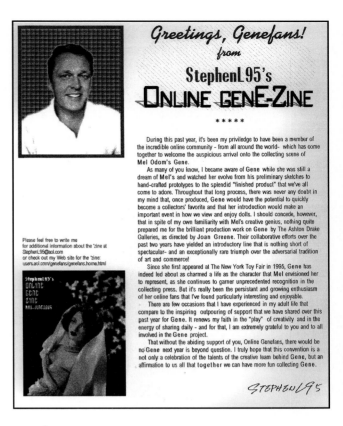

Stephen Long Puts Gene Online

Stephen Long was looking forward to seeing the *Gene* dolls produced. He felt that it was an opportunity for collectors to own a piece of Mel's art at an affordable price, and all the more exciting because "being three-dimensional, she was a pretty bold new direction for Mel to take as an incredibly accomplished illustrator." Stephen had seen the doll at Mel's and was "certain that it would be a sensational development." When the doll was not well received initially, he decided to try to get word to collectors about *Gene.*

Stephen had just purchased his first personal computer early in 1995 and was teaching himself to use it. Recognizing what a remarkable communication medium the Internet is, he explored online to find out about dolls. He found that "there was an unawareness among doll collectors, many of whom were feeling that they had lost a real sense of 'personal choice' and were being told by manufacturers what to believe about what was or what wasn't 'collectible'." Stephen formed a small online community of about 60 people in the summer of 1995. His goal was "to get information and nice images of *Gene* out" on the web and "to reinforce the purchase decision of collectors who were reluctant to jump into a new area of collecting."

Ashton-Drake did not have a web presence at that time, so collectors in search of information about *Gene* flocked to Stephen Long's monthy online newsletter. His "StephenL95'sOnline GenE-Zine" with photos of Mel, and information about the doll, drew more and more collectors. The original 60 people grew to 600, and then to a conservative estimate of 2,000 to 3,000 hits on his web page per month.

StephenL95's

ONLINE GENE-ZINE

The Online 'Zine For Gene Collectors Everywhere

November 1996

Celebrating Gene Marshall

Our 1996 Convention Issue!

"Green With Envy" by Gael Shapiro

Winner "Miss Gene, Beauty Queen - 1996"

The format of the GenE-Zine was a "hybridized electronic magazine" in which a series of 8-1/2 by 11 inch pages were posted as documents online that people could download and print out and save. Stephen featured a lot of photographs, usually taken by Steven Mays or Laura Meisner. "The first issue had six or seven pages," Stephen recalls, "and one and a half years later, the last had 16 pages." It had columns with news about conventions, articles about Mel and the designers, and profiles of the people online who had written about or designed for *Gene*. Each issue ended with a gossip column by a fictional character, Cora Harper. Cora was in the Hollywood mode of a Hedda or a Luella and she gave an "episodic snapshot" about *Gene's* activities, her career and fashions. Also included were articles about fan club activities. As a quarterly, the GenE-Zine was collectible in its own right.

For Stephen, the project was great for learning about computers as well as promoting Mel's project. He enjoyed corresponding with people from all around the world. Mel even now is "unwired" and to Steve the early response to the doll online was overwhelming. He tried to explain to Mel what a phenomenon *Gene* was and how quickly the web activity was growing surrounding the doll. One of the things he tried to underscore was the number of hits from around the world. With the web, *Gene's* fans were international.

Steve was "firmly convinced that the enthusiasm and unusual depth of reaction online" was remarkable. He says "I never saw people react on an intense personal level" like this before. "It was touching people on a visceral level." He believes that *Gene* connects to adult collectors, many of whom have no interest in juvenile or child-directed dolls, because she represents positive strength, humor, and the 'real adult' glamour and sophistication of her clothes." Stephen also thinks that *Gene* in a way is "a modern talisman that helps people get through emotional crises in their personal lives."

Stephen emphasizes that "The online community of *Gene's* fans is incredibly loyal and rapidly growing. Today there are now over 100 sites to be found on the World Wide Web where informtion and enthusiasm about *Gene* are shared among collectors." Stephen notes that "this is a long way from the days - not so long ago- when I would host online-chats with Mel. A few dozen of us fans would 'meet' in cyberspace and I would have Mel on the speakerphone, relaying his fans' questions to him and his answers back to them. It was a great, if crude, way to keep Mel in touch with collectors, which remains very important to him."

The Tide Begins to Turn

Sonia Rivera believes that three things helped the *Gene* project: "First the article that came out in *Barbie Bazaar* in January – that got people curious. Then four months later 'Holiday Magic' was announced as a limited edition costume, and a month later the retirement of 'Premier' was announced." She believes these were inspired strategies to attract the serious doll collectors.

The surge of interest in *Gene* made the decision-makers at Ashton-Drake take pause. The meeting with Mel to discuss dropping the renewal option was postponed because of the increase in sales – Ashton-Drake wanted to monitor what was happening. This encouraged everyone who was involved and they renewed efforts on *Gene's* behalf.

Mel's contacts with doll experts and authors such as John Darcy Noble and Beauregard Houston-Montgomery resulted in articles in doll publications. He also made a point to phone and thank retailers who had bought and advertised *Gene,* a personal touch that helped build support for the doll.

At Ashton-Drake in January 1996, Kate Dwyer, Director of New Business Development, recommended to the General Manager that *Gene* should be given one last chance. She suggested that Joan Greene head a spin-off group to give *Gene* the attention that Mel and Joan had been requesting. That group consisted of Michael Boyd, representing marketing (who later went with Nordstrom), Barbara White, as copywriter, and Frank Rotundo, for development. By the spring of 1996 their new strategies and the repositioning of *Gene* were paying off. Collectors were finding *Gene* through the "new look" ads that were appearing regularly in the collector doll publications.

In July 1996, Linda Masterson requested to be moved into the *Gene* group as Director. Because she had over 25 years of agency and brand marketing experience, she recognized that *Gene* had the makings of a brand. The excitement of working on what was to become Ashton-Drake's first branded product brought Linda enthusiastically into the *Gene* program.

Linda explains, "Ashton-Drake, like all direct mail companies, sells products. They specialize in solo offers. They sell dolls or plates to collectors. *Gene* is a brand – clearly a brand with a passionate following. The idea behind *Gene* is to understand that there is a collection."

With the different approach in the marketing of the doll and the revision of their advertising, Ashton-Drake realized that there was some interest in *Gene.* Hesitating to "pull the plug outright," they decided to go ahead with a new line to be shown at the 1996 Toy Fair, and added two dolls and three costumes.

"Once we started applying the brand marketing approach," explains Masterson, "we expanded the line so that it started being viewed as a collection and not just a doll to buy." They changed the advertising so that one *Gene* doll was shown with two or three costumes and an accessory.

Stephen Long discontinued his *Genezine* in the Spring of 1997 because of the heavy demands. "There was a lot of flock tending. I was getting 90 E-mails a day. It was turning into a full-time job!" But he realizes how important the Internet was for *Gene.* "The Internet molds public impressions, like for the movie stars of the past." He hopes that Ashton-Drake will put more emphasis on the net. "I cultivated *Gene's* image and I had no resources." He goes on to say "my satisfaction is knowing that fans have insisted on the *Gene* doll and made it a success. It is a true, *bona fide* success that the people have made.

That's an exception, the rule is that the manufacturer dictates (what is successful)."

In retrospect, with *Gene*'s current popularity, Mel Odom, Ashton-Drake, and all of us who collect *Gene* can only be grateful that the project was not discontinued. Perhaps the old saying about true love never running smoothly applies to the *Gene* project! Joan Greene devoutly believes that "Mel loved *Gene* alive."

Mel says "I've learned that people pay dearly for everything they get. These fashion models who are discovered and become overnight sensations, somewhere down the line pay dearly. There is no free ride in life. You get, you give. I was putting so much into this, that I always felt I had to be getting things out of it as well. Just the laws of physics required that. And that it came from a point of love in me, a love of many different things. I believe this to be a tremendous strength in any endeavor."

Mel goes on to say, "I thought I was doing *Gene* for all the right reasons and …somebody would recognize that, and I would succeed." He goes on to emphasize that "Thinking you will succeed and succeeding are two very different things. It is a daily challenge to look at this and continue with it, and keep it at the high level it started. Even when you've done well, you don't want to make stupid mistakes.

Gene's Supporters

In addition to Mel, Joan, and the others who had worked on the *Gene* project, there were others who from the moment they saw the first *Gene* line were believers.

As early as Toy Fair in February 1995

Arthur and Hermione Weston with Mel and Brittany Jacoves.

some retailers were taking note of *Gene*. Two such retailers are Arthur and Hermione Weston, the owners of Weston's Limited Editions in New Jersey. The Westons first saw the *Gene* doll at the 1995 Toy Fair in New York. They were "taken with it - she had a different, beautiful face" and felt "the clothing was exceptional."

The Westons also admired the fact that there was a creative and charismatic artist presenting the doll. As dealers, they recognized what an asset the artist's personal appearances and signings can be for the promotion of a doll. *Gene* "came with credentials," in their words. The Westons saw the doll as a credible challenge to that *other* fashion doll, and their first ad in *Doll Reader* was bold enough to state: "Move over *Barbie*®, here comes *Gene!*"

Another supporter from "day one" is Isobel Weill, owner of the doll shop "Best of Everything." She liked that "*Gene* was a sophisticated doll. Her larger size showed off the clothes." Even more importantly, "When collectors bought an outfit they got the complete package – all of the accessories, the jewelry, the hose, the hat – everything they needed at a reasonable price." Weill also likes the quality of the vinyl on *Gene*, "Ashton-Drake did a wonderful job on the vinyl – it looks just like porcelain."

Arthur Weston thinks, as a dealer who has been active in the secondary market over the years, that "what really galvanized the whole thing was the announcement that 'Premiere' was closing. We had another 100 coming in (when the announcement was made) and decided to save them for an ad with a photo of 'Premiere' and the statement "Just suppose you had bought the first *Barbie* ever retired?" When the ad was published Weston was travelling. His first inkling of the ad's success was that his calls to the shop wouldn't go through – the lines were clogged with collectors ordering "Premiere."

Another dealer who began carrying the *Gene* line that first year is Margo Rana. Well-known as a *Barbie*® authority, Rana agrees that *Gene* was slow to catch on. She had a "Premiere" in her shop for close to a year, but when the retirement was announced, it sold immediately. Now, she says "*Gene* is nuclear!" Many of her customers are former *Barbie*® collectors. Those who can justify and afford continuing on with both dolls, collect both.

Rana believes that the limited editions "are what drives the market, what keeps the interest going."

In talking about limited editions, Weston says it is interesting to note that the 2,000 limited edition of "Holiday Magic" took a while to sell out when it was introduced in the fall of 1996, but when the 5,000 "Blossoms in the Snow" came out, it sold much more quickly. "In 1998, the 7,500 'Ransom in Red' sold out immediately.

Dan Miller of *Miller's Fashion Doll* magazine wrote that *Gene* is "America's hottest new collectible fashion doll." He believes that "*Gene* is the first legitimate competition to *Barbie*®." Miller's business involves observing collectors, and he sees *Gene* as possessing the momentum that *Barbie*® used to possess. Since his magazine expanded its newstand coverage he has noticed a dramatic increase in collectors calling in to subscribe because of the *Gene* coverage.

Sonia Rivera sent out her first *Gene Scene* magazine in October 1996. Sonia would call Mel and Ashton-Drake for information, and would answer questions from collectors. She believes that "part of the pull was that collectors were sick of dolls in boxes they couldn't do anything with. They can take *Gene* out of the box and redress her. That brings out the little girl in you. It is like going back to the original *Cissy* – she had rings, necklaces – *Gene* went back to that."

Margo Rana agrees. "One of the most attractive things to collectors is that they are encouraged to play with *Gene*. They can take the doll out of the box and dress and redress it." She says that it has been drummed into collectors to not take their dolls out of the box, but by doing that "they are not experiencing the fun of playing with the doll."

Isobel Weill, too, thinks that *Gene* is appealing to collectors because they can have so much fun with her. "*Gene* is an adult play toy that is meant to be undressed and redressed. Collectors love the accessories and clothes."

A dealer who turned down the invitation to carry *Gene* in the beginning, is *Barbie*® expert Marl Davidson. "I didn't want to diversify, and I didn't like her at first," she says. "I kept looking at her at shows and studying her. She is the kind of doll you notice, but it takes time to fall in love with her." Drawn to the quality of the clothes and the accessories - "everything is impeccable"- Davidson changed her mind. Not only does she sell *Gene* dolls, but says that they have had extraordinary success with her customers in Japan, South Africa, Germany, Spain, Portugal, and other countries.

Davidson thinks that some of *Gene's* appeal is that "people are so enamoured with the 1940s – they love the look." She recalls her mother taking her to the movies as a child. "The clothes, and all those hats, gloves, and purses were dazzling. They made a big impression on me... *Gene* takes so well to those clothes – she is everybody's dream girl. She looks good in everything!"

Davidson says "I cannot tell you it was love at first sight, with me and *Gene*. She was too mature, too tall, and almost too sexy. As time passed, however, I couldn't help but notice that it was those qualities that made her divine. Here is a mature sexy woman, exploding into the world of teen fashion models and

Mary Hennessy of FAO Schwarz receives a "Destiny" from student designer Mark Esposito while Rick Tinberg, President and CEO of The Bradford Exchange, looks on.

winning the hearts of collectors everywhere. They love her because she reminds them of a time when doll clothes were classy, sophisticated and well made. A time when dolls were able to be taken from their boxes and proudly displayed, because they were judged on the quality of their production, not their box. So maybe it wasn't love at first sight ... like *Gene*, it was a more grown up, adult, over time affection that will surely be around as long as she will... and that's forever."

An important supporter of *Gene* is FAO Schwarz. Mary Hennessy, for the last four years the buyer for girl's toys at the FAO headquarters in New York, says that this year they are rolling out the *Gene* line to their entire chain and that the top 20 or so stores will carry the entire *Gene* line. Mary sees the *Gene* doll as becoming a staple for them.

Mary agrees that "*Gene* is exactly what people are looking for. The detailing on the dolls is exceptional. The history and story around Gene Marshall is intriguing. The price point is inviting for collectors and for people of all ages. The doll can be enjoyed because collectors are encouraged to take it out of the box. We like to support a doll that people can touch." Mary also says that *Gene* is different from the other dolls they carry "because she has a more mature appeal. A smaller percentage of people are buying the doll for children and some 12 to 14 year olds are buying it."

FAO Schwarz has also offered exclusive *Gene* dolls that Mary says "are doing very well. These exclusives are an up and coming piece of our doll business. We're big *Gene* fans." Their relationship with Ashton-Drake draws praise from Mary "Joan and Linda have great flair and Mel has made three appearances. He is so personable and warm. At the events, the *Gene* Team are so excited – it's contagious." She goes on to say that "Ashton-Drake is smart about growing their business. They have high standards, they're not greedy. They are a small group putting together this line. They're a cohesive group, a very nice group – very accessible."

Mary Hennessy ends with an important point: "Everything enhances the story of Gene Marshall. They won't make it if *Gene* wouldn't have embraced it. Everything is in keeping with her story." It is a versatile doll, Mary says "because of the roles *Gene* can play. Each doll takes on a different personality, even though they all have the same face sculpt."

Isobel Weill gives the final word, "*Gene* has staying power. As long as Ashton-Drake continues to give the collectors the kind of quality and outfits they have up until now, *Gene* will last. She has the chance of being round a long, long time."

The fans concur. At the 1998 Toy Fair, Ashton-Drake's press release stated that "Over 400 people waited for hours in the rain to see (*Gene*) at a recent signing in California.

Magazines run dozens of articles on her, and her web site receives 65,000 visits a month." Isobel Weill describes Mel's last signing for her at the Rothman Center. "People stood in line all day long to buy *Gene* dolls and outfits for Mel to sign, yet they were so relaxed. No one complained about the long wait."

A *New York Times* article by Frank DeCaro states "*Gene* Marshall is a hit on the collectibles circuit, with more than half a million dolls and costumes sold in the three years since her debut. She has spawned *Gene* fan clubs, *Genezines*, *Gene* Web pages and annual collectors' conventions. (And) A column devoted to her runs monthly in *Collecting Figures* magazine."

After a rocky beginning, *Gene* is finally being accorded the adulation and attention a movie star celebrity deserves! *G*

Some of the Gene Team members are pictured at the Rosemont International Collector's Show: Frank Rotundo, Linda Masterson, Mel Odom, "Incognito" model, Wendy Solomon, and Beth Maxwell.

Joan Greene; Don Vaccarello, Vice President, General Manager, The Ashton-Drake Galleries; and Linda Masterson.

Rick Tinberg, President and CEO, The Bradford Group.

The *Gene* Team. Front: Linda Masterson, Director; Chris Gagnon, former Marketing Manager; Frank Rotundo, Associate Product Development Manager. Back: Wendy Solomon, Customer Service Representative; Beth Maxwell, Retail Marketing Manager; Joan Greene, Team Leader, Senior Product Development Manager; and Diane Ladley, Senior Copywriter.

The Gene Team
at Ashton-Drake Galleries

Joan Greene
Team Leader & Senior Product Development Manager

Mel Odom said "If I am *Gene's* dad, then Joan Greene is her mom in the dedication and the amount of time she has given to this." Joan was hired by Ashton-Drake in May, 1994.

Mel had already presented the *Gene* doll in February of that year, but the project was still in a portfolio. *Gene* was completely different from the porcelain baby dolls that were Ashton-Drake's specialty, and they were looking for a person to guide the *Gene* undertaking. Joan says, her forte "is looking at something and figuring out how to make it 5,000 times" which made her ideal for the project.

Taking the job with Ashton-Drake meant selling her home in sunny California and moving to the harsher climate of Chicago. She had been hired for her entrepreneurial spirit and combined right-brain, left-brain skills. The fact that Ashton-Drake had purchased the license for *Gene* and had not started to work on her was the challenge that kept Joan going. She says she loves beginnings – the birthing of a project with all the ups and downs made every day exciting

and new and kept her from being homesick for California.

The company was expert at producing porcelain dolls, but had never produced a vinyl product. Joan was initially shown the plaster prototype of the doll, some costumes and the movie star story that Mel had written. She was struck with the idea – that *Gene* represented the American dream. She felt that many American women live by the philoso-

phy that if you have a dream, and work hard enough, it can be achieved. That, Joan felt, was part of the reason *Gene* is so compelling.

Joan's background is in product development. She came to Ashton-Drake experienced in developing dolls, teddy bears, and

miniature toys. She had developed a line "Victorian memories" for Hallmark cards, and in 1981 had started one of the first stores devoted to collectible teddy bears. The store, which was originally in Berkeley and later moved to Ghiradelli Square in San Francisco, carried handmade bears. Joan sent out a direct response catalog for the artists' bears, which was very innovative for that product at that time.

At Ashton-Drake, in addition to *Gene*, Joan has managed the development of many other new products, including Disney dolls, McDonald's collectibles, a Princess Diana doll, a Revlon doll, and with her experience with teddy bears, was the obvious person to start the Ashton-Drake teddy bear division.

Her love of the teddy bears led to her writing articles for the various bear collectors' magazines and to co-author a book *The Complete Book of Teddy Bears*.

Collecting antique toys has been a life-long hobby, especially doll furniture and boxed board game sets along with the teddy bears. "Because I'm a collector I understand the passion around collecting *Gene*," Joan says. "You name it and I collect it! I tend to collect old things, and *Gene* has a quality and

a sense that seems timeless – I love that." She goes on to explain, "with an antique there was a person who loved it and helped it survive." She feels that by owning an antique, a person is owning a piece of that time. She thinks that *Gene* has that same quality. Part of Joan's contribution is "I add that sensitivity and love for what has been before, and an understanding of the time."

Joan maintains that part of *Gene's* importance is that she reflects women's roles after the Great Depression. During World War II women came into their own and worked outside the home. "The Rosie Riviters were the role models, they are why we work today. Women realized that they could do anything and that is part of what *Gene* is about."

On first seeing the *Gene* prototype, Joan says "I knew we had something special!" After her work was done on the other Ashton-Drake programs, she would stay and work on *Gene*. *Gene* became her extracurricular activity, partly because she was still new to Chicago, but mostly because "I always knew *Gene* would be a winner!"

Greene says that *Gene* mirrored her own dreams, "the dreams of a kid who grew up on a farm in Mississippi." She remembered her father telling her that "the most important things were relationships" and "if you dream it, you can have it."

Joan knew as a youngster that her ambitions did not include staying on the farm near Louisville, Mississippi, a town of 5,000 people. Books and art were her way out. She kept scrapbooks of famous people and places to go, and read virtually every book in the local library. She was imaginative, "I lived inside my head and was in a fantasy world when helping out on the farm."

Joan earned a bachelor's of Fine Arts at the Mississippi University for Women, and later a master's degree. Her undergrad school, "The W" is the oldest state supported college for women in America. It started during the Civil War and she likens *Gene's* heritage as similar to many of the young women at that university. "We were required to take elocution and poise classes, like *Gene* as a starlet would be expected to take as part of her Hollywood training." Joan recalls the graduation ceremony at which each woman carried a magnolia, each flower a part of a long chain of magnolias which the junior class by tradition stays up all night to weave. It is easy to picture *Gene* in that scene!

When Joan was a senior in college she saved enough for a trip to New York City. She wanted to hear Norman Vincent Peale speak on the Power of Positive Thinking and to attend the Easter brunch at the Plaza Hotel, which to her, was a "quintessential bit of elegance." After working with the *Gene* doll for six months, Joan came up with the marketing scheme to throw a big party for *Gene* and to "introduce" her to her fans at the Plaza.

When Joan first came to Ashton-Drake, she and Mel had not yet met in person, they worked together via phone. She first called him to establish how far along he was with the doll. Before long, they spoke numerous times every day. She says she believes "the most he called was 14 times in one day!"

When the original sculpture finally came to Joan she had to turn it into something the factories could produce. Working with an engineer in Chicago she managed the development of the prototype models. Refinements were made to the original. Then Joan, consulting with an engineer in Asia, worked out the details of the jointing.

When the duplicate prototypes were sent to Asia, it was Joan's brainchild to have

Three examples of the 50 Showgirls made for the FAO Schwarz opening in Las Vegas. Joan made 48 of them!

Joan and Mel congratulate a Young Designer of America winner at Santa Barbara.

the lines segregated with workers who made the doll or the costumes work on nothing but *Gene* to maintain the high quality. With the costumes, in particular, a "ton of hand sewing" is necessary, such as hand stitching on sequins. With "Night in Versailles" Joan went to the factory and taught the workers how to do ribbon embroidery. "For that kind of attention to detail, we need to have dedicated workers," says Joan. The dolls and the costumes that come on the dolls are made in a factory in China. The costumes that are packaged separately are made mostly in the Philippines.

Joan gives credit to the design people who have worked on *Gene*, because, she says, "they bring all of the skills they have from their own life to the project." In her own case, Joan tells of learning hand sewing from her grandmother MaAnnie, who is now 93 years old. Joan recalls asking MaAnnie to sew something for her *Barbie®* doll to wear to

President Kennedy's funeral, since the doll didn't have appropriate mourning clothes.

Joan's primary job as *Gene* Team Leader/Senior Product Development Manager consists of managing the development of all original prototypes and overseeing the product through production. In addition, she and Linda Masterson now work together in the strategy and business development for *Gene*. When it looked as if the *Gene* project might be discontinued, Joan was asked to head up the spin-off group that changed the way *Gene* was marketed. They introduced *Gene's* first retirement, planned her first limited edition costume, and repositioned the look of *Gene* photography.

Although Joan continues to manage the development of new products, oversees production and team staff, marketing, creative approaches, and travels for *Gene,* she says what she loves about *Gene* is the feeling that she is working for a really big star. "My

64

job is to make *Gene* always look beautiful and authentic to her story, and to keep her fans happy. Glamour is hard work, but *Gene* is worth it!"

According to Mel "One of the keys to *Gene's* success is that both Joan and I come from small southern towns and understand the strength of a fantasy." *G*

Linda Masterson

Director

Linda understands the collector's mentality, because she herself is a collector. She loves antiques and collects vintage costume jewelry, dresser jars, hand-painted porcelain and glass, and Bakelite. Her home is decorated with eclectic antiques, but until she became associated with *Gene*, she had not collected dolls.

Originally from Bay Village, near Cleveland, Ohio, Linda Masterson was the eldest of eight children. She gravitated to Chicago and spent 15 years working in the Ketchum Advertising Agency. By the time she left, she was Senior Vice President and Creative Director. From there, she went to Enesco as Director of Marketing for Precious Moments. It was a familiar line since she had been working on the Precious Moments account for four years while at Ketchum. After two years at Enesco, she was recruited by Ashton-Drake to work in New Development on new business ventures.

A week after coming to Ashton-Drake, in February 1996, she attended the New York Toy Fair. *Gene* was the product of a different Ashton-Drake group, but Linda recalls being mesmerized by the doll. The following July Linda was moved over to the *Gene* division. Along with Joan Greene, Michael Boyd, Barbara White and Frank Rotundo, she focused on rethinking the entire *Gene* strategy.

As the Director, Linda's responsibility is to run the "*Gene* Team" group. She sets the direction and strategy for the brand as a whole. She and Joan work very closely together to decide the concept, where they will go, the philosophy, and how big and how fast they should grow the *Gene* brand. She also is responsible for the people, for advertising, for support materials, and collateral, and, of course, the bottom line.

The decisions made can have a great effect on a product. For example, Linda says "The packaging for *Gene* is deliberately not glamorous. There is no benefit to keeping *Gene* in a box. Since it isn't a view-through box to display her in, more collectors are taking her out." She laughs that NRFB and MIB should be put into the circle signs with diagonal lines through them to abolish that kind of collecting.

Linda shared the results of a recent

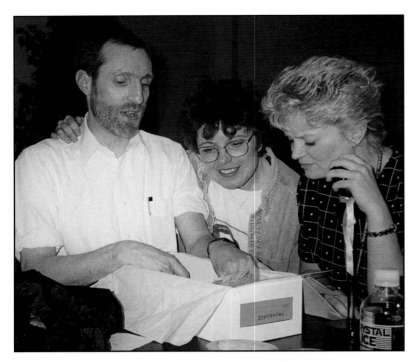

Frank Rotundo, Linda Masterson, and Beth Maxwell.

average *Gene* collector has five dolls, five costumes, and two accessories. Many call themselves beginning collectors. The great majority want more dolls, more costumes, and especially, more accessories such as hats, jewelry, furniture, and so on. "They are in love with *Gene* and want her world to expand. They want more things to make her more real."

Linda outlined how the *Gene* products are chosen. Initially ideas come from Mel. When the collection is planned, the group meets and reviews what has been successful in the current line as to the styles and colors of the clothes. They "literally make a grid showing what we have, what we need to fill in. We want to deliver a really broad range. We do a lot of analyzing and then present the results to Mel." It takes at least a day to discuss everything with Mel, and at the end they have formulated the line plan – the number of dolls, costumes, how many limited editions, what accessories, and so on for the next year.

Linda emphasizes that the *Gene* Team works in a partnership with Mel and that Ashton-Drake has a long-term licensing agreement with him. He is always a part of the strategic planning and works closely with Joan on a day-to-day basis. His genius, says Linda "is envisioning what he wants. Ours at Ashton-Drake is in making it happen. If Mel can dream it, we can make it happen if it is the right thing to do. We don't want to compromise the level of quality."

She mentions that the long-term plans include licensing to other companies for products relating to *Gene* – cinema and books being a logical extension. Their plans are very encompassing, with the emphasis now on expanding to other life style products that reflect the nostalgia of the 1940s and 50s.

Like many others who are attracted to

survey, the first lifestyle tracking study of *Gene* collectors. The survey indicated that most *Gene* shoppers bought dolls retail and that they are younger than the average Ashton-Drake customers - most are "baby boomers." The *Gene* fans are more affluent, better educated, and less likely to have a child at home than other Ashton-Drake buyers. They tend to be interested in artistic pursuits – many of them collect antiques, and many watch A&E or PBS, for example. They are people who don't collect for nurturing, unlike many of the buyers of the baby dolls.

Collectors appreciate the quality associated with *Gene*, love the romantic, glamorous, nostalgic era she represents. "The 1940s in particular," Linda says, "are remembered as a simpler time. It was an era where women were revered and glamorous. The strong movie stars of the day were women. And the movies had happy endings." That Golden Age of Hollywood is a strong attractant.

The research also told them that the

Gene, but who don't consider themselves doll collectors, Linda has her favorites. "I have a 'Premiere' on top of my bookcase. She holds a *Gene* shopping bag filled with flowers and a teddy bear, and draped behind her is a small fur. She has a table, a dresser next to her. I love to watch my '*Gene* thing' grow." She is also fond of 'Midnight Romance' - "it is very elegant," and "I love 'Destiny' and think it is mesmerizing, but I'm not sure why."

She tells that the new marketing group for *Gene* attended an orientation meeting. All non-collectors, they were offered a *Gene* for their offices. They all wanted a doll, and each had different favorites.

Linda also tells a story about her bosses, Vice President and General Manager at Ashton-Drake, Don Vaccarello, who was not impressed with *Gene* in the beginning but who is now one of *Gene's* most ardent fans, and Bradford President and CEO Rich Tinberg. "Incognito" was originally supposed to be a costume, but when it was shown on a doll at the Executive Approval Meeting where the budget for the year was presented – a very businesslike meeting normally, Vaccarello and Tinberg halted the meeting raving over "Incognito." That's why, she says, instead of four, there are five dolls in the line this year! Tinberg believes strongly that *Gene* will become one of the icons of the doll business. *G*

Beth Maxwell

Retail Marketing Manager

The Retail Marketing Manager for the *Gene* Team is Beth Maxwell. She is originally from Davenport, Iowa, and has a background in advertising and communication. Beth had 20 years of retail experience with J.C. Penney. When their regional offices con-

solidated, she moved to the Chicago area. When she was offered another job with J.C. Penney that meant relocating, Beth began looking around for jobs in the Chicago area. Answering a classified in the newspaper, she was hired by Ashton-Drake at the end of 1997.

Beth relates a history of collecting one item and then moving on to another, and names collections of Precious Moments figurines and Disney collectibles. Beth's responsibilities include show coordination, and being a liaison between retailers and Ashton-Drake, and doing store training.

She especially enjoys "meeting the *Gene* collectors at shows and hearing from them what they love about *Gene*." She also enjoys the fact that in working the shows, *Gene* never gets boring. "She looks different in the different booths. The hairstyles especially can change the way she looks. When you see *Gene* in person she draws you in. Each day you see more and notice different details." *G*

Diane Ladley
Senior Copywriter

The Senior Copywriter for the *Gene* Team is Diane Ladley. Born and raised in Naperville, Illinois, Diane loved to write even as a child. She won a newspaper award for one of her pieces, but never dreamed she could make a living by writing. She went to DePaul University in Indiana, and after college went into sales.

With 12 years experience working in ad agencies as a copywriter, Diane came to Ashton-Drake and worked on the regular baby dolls before joining the *Gene* Team in 1997. Along with authoring the story lines and collector card stories, Ladley writes for catalogs, ads for newspapers, and dealer point of purchase materials.

As a little girl, Diane liked horses, and the dolls she played with always had heroic roles – they were "dressed in togas and fought evil." She was never a collector, but admits to falling for *Gene*'s nostalgic appeal. She has half a dozen *Gene* dolls, and even searched for "Midnight Romance" on the secondary market. She had to own one since that is her favorite *Gene* story so far.

The "Smart Set" story is also appeal-ing to her, because of the "darkly atmospher-ic thriller role" that *Gene* plays in it. "Cameo," she says, creates a mood and touches the heart. It is a story that Diane worked on shortly after her mother died, so it is especially poignant for her.

Diane enjoys working with Mel on the biography and timeline of *Gene*. She loves movies, old and new, and finds *Gene*'s time period fascinating. She loves to do research on the 1940s and 50s era. The first tale she worked on with Mel is the one for "White Hyacinth." The copywriter for the earlier sto-ries was Barbara White.

Diane says that Mel first comes up with the story lines and then she does research to find out the accurate details. Occasionally they have a great idea for a story that is ruled out by historic reality. She gives the "Night at Versailles" as an example. The original story line was going to be about a glittering ball held at Versailles. Unfortunately, on fact checking, she found that Versailles was not restored until a year after the event was to have taken place, so the story had to be changed so that *Gene* would attend a party to encourage the restoration of the palace.

An important part of Diane's job is to make sure the timeline and story line don't have conflicts. One example where a fact had to be changed between the printing of the first batch of collector cards and succeeding ones was "El Morocco." On the original card, *Gene*'s father's 50th birthday is mentioned. Because another segment of Gene's history included a mention of his part in the war effort during World War I, his age had to be changed to 60 on the collector cards for the El Morocco birthday party.

Diane likes story telling so much that she does it in her spare time, too. She is a part-time professional story teller for children, at festivals and in schools. Her specialty is ghost stories. *G*

Frank Rotundo

Associate Product Development Manager

Frank Rotundo came to work at Ashton-Drake in 1995 as Joan Greene's assistant in new business development. "Since I was not from the doll industry, I was easy to train!" His background is heavy in manufacturing and specialty items, so he is "aware of how something can be manufactured and the time schedule." He says that the *Gene* program is nice because the collectors are so patient. "They may really want something, but they are willing to wait." That isn't true, he explains, "for the people who want nuclear valves for submarines – they get testy there!"

He was brought in when there was a concern about the longevity of the *Gene* doll and the only people on the "*Gene* Team" were Joan and Mel. Frank began as a "temp," packing boxes for Joan. He recalls the attempt to be positive: "We were telling people (*Gene* was) the most fabulous thing. We were acting as if it was already successful."

Because Joan does a lot of travelling, Frank's main responsibility is acting as the liaison between her and the factories. He handles the samples that are sent back and forth and works to keep everything on schedule.

Constant searching for the right fabrics is a challenge. Because the size and scale of the fabrics are so important, Frank spends a lot of time trying to find substitutes for fabrics that have been discontinued or that are antique. He says wool is especially difficult. Frank tells about the time he tried to find a brocade that was used on a design submitted by one of the student designers. After investigating, he discovered that the fabric was from a Korean mourning garment and that it hadn't been made since the Korean War.

He mentions "Afternoon Off" and "Good-Bye New York" as "having three or four 'facelifts' with new fabrics." Because of the scale of *Gene's* clothes, the amounts of any one fabric needed may be relatively small; but getting it just right is so important that fabrics are often purchased in the United States and sent to Asia. Frank handles all those details. He mentions that at one point they thought it would be fun to try a large houndstooth for the "Good-Bye New York" skirt, but there was a lot of wastage because of matching the large print so they reverted back to the smaller pattern.

Another challenge, Frank says, is in communicating with the people in the factories for whom English is a second language. Coming from a family that is second generation Italian on one side and second generation German on the other, he says that frequent rephrasing is his habit when he is talking to people not proficient in English – he is accustomed to doing that with relatives. He notes that using any kind of slang in dealing with the factories could be a problem – a term like "crunching up" might be taken literally.

Like the other *Gene* Team members, Frank is from a small town, Carpentersville,

Illinois, located 60 miles from Chicago. He thinks that the shared small town experience is valuable for the group since in many cases going back home can be "like stepping back into the 1940s." His hometown, like many, had a post war boom when buildings such as banks, soda fountains, and bowling alleys were built. These buildings, still in use, impart a period flavor.

Frank loves things from the 1930s, 40s, and 50s such as the clothes and music. His mother grew up during that period and he says that there was strong belief then that anyone, like Lana Turner, might be discovered at the corner drugstore and turned into a movie star. "Women had to be ready to be snapped up by a producer to be a movie star. They knew the etiquette and bought magazines to learn about the stars" so that they would be prepared when it happened.

The *Gene* doll embodies all the glamour and hope of a time gone by. *G*

Wendy Solomon
Customer Service Representative

Wendy Solomon is the Customer Service Representative who answers all of the questions that people call in to ask about *Gene*. She is the one who has to answer "Why did the lips go from matte to shiny?" or "Why doesn't a lady of her stature wear underpants in the lingerie set?" or "When will *Gene* get a boyfriend?" or "Why is the fabric in 'Afternoon Off' different from the picture?"

Wendy was "smitten with *Gene*" from the beginning, when she came to work at Ashton-Drake in March of 1997. Three months later she moved to the *Gene* Team. She is especially interested in the movie aspect of *Gene*. She has worked as a programmer for the Chicago Underground Film Festival since its inception five years ago.

She enjoys talking with *Gene* fans and says that she has become friends with many of the customers who call in with questions or concerns. "The clients need someone to be meticulous. They won't take 'I don't know' for an answer! She tells of one *Gene* collector who owns six "Blue Goddess" dolls because he kept running across examples in which the curls were slightly different. Wendy says that "the *Gene* fans are very passionate because she represents so many different things, sometimes even themselves." *G*

Gene Team members in front of a New York City bus that carries a Gene banner during Toy Fair 1999. From left to right: Frank Rotundo, Beth Maxwell, Julie Najawicz, Dee Golfinopoulos, Linda Masterson, and Joan Greene.

Ashton-Drake's Freelance Talent

Dolly Cipolla

A freelance seamstress-costume designer for Ashton-Drake, Dolly has been working on the *Gene* costumes since the beginning. Her job is to sew between three to six prototypes of each of *Gene's* outfits and to create the patterns for production in the factory in Asia.

Dolly's training was at the International Academy of Merchandise and Design, Ltd. in Chicago. After design school, she had a line of clothes in the Chicago department store Carson, Pirie, and Scott. Later, she

Dolly Cipolla is the mother of three young daughters, and by the end of August 1998, a baby son, so it seems appropriate that she is known for sewing tiny garments. Except that the tiny dresses that she makes are not for children, they are for dolls.

had a business creating one-of-a-kind dresses for ladies on the North Shore in Chicago. She also worked directly with the clients of a costume clothing designer, and worked for a clothing manufacturer preparing garments for factory assembly.

Dolly has always loved design. She lived in the country as a child. Growing up in Wisconsin, 25 minutes outside of Fond du Lac, she went to grade school in a class of seven children that was taught by her sister. Dolly never played with dolls as a child, but loves *Gene* because her clothes are real fashions in miniature. "It is so challenging to make her fashions look real in a miniature scale." She also likes working with dolls as models rather than people because "the dolls don't talk back. They just stand there!"

When a new design is approved by Ashton-Drake, Dolly meets with Joan Greene

"Lady Liberty" was one-of-a-kind auction doll costumed by Dolly Cipolla for the second Gene Convention.

or Frank Rotundo to review the details and discuss the creation of the duplicates. Her task is to duplicate the artist's original several times. "The designers' work is brilliant!" Dolly says. But her biggest challenge is to adapt the clothes into a form that allows them to be mass-produced by an assembly line. "The duplicate prototypes must look exactly alike," she stresses.

The garments that come form the students are more difficult to work with than those from the designers, since the students aren't required to supply a pattern. With their designs, she is supplied the sewn garment. "Sometimes," Dolly admits, "it is hard to be sure what the students intend. When asked to do the prototyping of those she also has to interpret the garment into pattern form while staying loyal to what the student was thinking.

In some cases others on the *Gene* design team are asked to interpret for the student. For example, Tim Kennedy reproduced "The King's Daughter."

Dolly enjoys the variety of fabrics and the high-fashion aspect of the designs for *Gene.* She says that when she worked on clothes for baby dolls there was "a lot of pink gingham, and with that, there are a limited number of places to put the pink bows!"

She says that "Midnight Romance" was so challenging, but really worked well. "Crescendo" was also formidable – "it has linings, some things pleated and some not," but looks elegant.

Unlike the New York designers who drape the costumes, Dolly's work requires drafting. "To make an outfit fit and look good on a doll is difficult, when you work that tiny it is challenging. With a pattern that has a lot of pieces it is more challenging because you can't be off by even a sixteenth of an inch" she says. As she is always reminded by the Development staff at Ashton-Drake, "with *Gene* you want that wonderful figure to show when it is dressed. In 'Sparkling Seduction' the first prototype I did looked flat chested. It is all a matter of where you put those (seam) lines. Gene looks really wonderful in princess-style dresses." *G*

Etta Foran

A teddy bear artist for Ashton-Drake since 1995, Etta Foran is the logical person to design *Gene's* dogs "Dottie" and "Dasheill." However, she has also made the prototypes of *Gene's* shoes, some of *Gene's* jewelry, hatboxes, and other props.

Etta has three *Gene* dolls at present. "After I started handling her, she grew on me. I'm not a doll person, I always liked the stuffed animals." She collects Steiff dogs, artists' teddy bears, pepsi collectibles and pocket dragons and "likes antiques."

Doing the shoes for *Gene* "just happened out of the blue," Etta says. She had worked with Joan Greene on the teddy bear program and had worked on props for different projects such as miniature cups for McDonalds.

For the shoes, she is usually given a prototype shoe from the designer or sent a piece of fabric that the shoes are supposed to match. In that case she paints the shoe to match the material. She laughs about one shade of green that was seemingly impossible to find in a paint color. She ended up taking a swatch of material to the paint store to have a quart of paint custom mixed. It may have been more than was needed for three small pairs of shoes, but it matched the fabric exactly.

"The shoes that have ribbons up the leg don't take long," Etta says, but "the suede shoes have to have patterns made" and are really time-intensive. "Between Frank and me, we get it right."

She usually does all of the shoes for the *Gene* dolls shown at Toy Fair, and she also made 50 pairs of shoes for the Las Vegas FAO Schwartz opening's one-of-a-kind dolls.

Etta has also become an expert at making tiny rhinestone bracelets and other jewelry to *Gene* scale. Again, she normally is sent the prototype, and then duplicates it. She says she is "amazed at how good they are in Asia" at mass producing the things they are sent. "It takes me so long to do the things."

Making the dogs was more what Etta is accustomed to doing. From Joliet, Illinois, she has designed and made teddy bears for 14 years. Most of her bears are between eight and 20 inches, are jointed mohair and made in limited editions. Because Joan was familiar with Etta's plush animals, she asked her to make a pair of Scottie terriers for *Gene*, "with short legs and fat faces." Adjusting the originals to be slightly higher, Etta then made the sets of prototypes necessary to have them produced.

Other *Gene* props by Etta are the chopsticks for "Mandarin Mood," painting and lining the prototype trunks, and making the "Hi-Fi" album cover and record. "The record was fun to figure out. A clock maker showed me how to get the record perfectly round."

She is proud of the work she does for the *Gene* line. "The details are something else!" She says that Joan is a "stickler for detail. Gee, I don't know where she comes up with her ideas!" *G*

Steven Mays
Gene's Photographer

In 1995, Steven Mays and Mel, who first met 25 years ago, ran into each other at a neighborhood photo lab in New York City after several years of being out of touch. It was a fateful meeting – Mel had a lot to tell about *Gene*, his new fashion doll, that had already appeared in her first catalog, but had not been flattered in the photographs. Steven had a photography studio and during the conversation they decided to work together on some photos to see how glamorous they could make *Gene* look.

Steven, who has a degree in English Literature from the University of Virginia, taught English at a Junior College for five years before going to London to study photography. One of his students knew Mel and suggested that Steven look him up in London.

The years that Steven was teaching "were an experimental phase," he says. Each year he took on a different kind of project – one year he experimented with drama and produced a play, another year he delved into art history, and finally he ended up working with black and white photography which culminated in a one-man show in Birmingham, Alabama. In London, he studied theatrical

"Since he and Mel worked on the initial photographs of Gene, Steven has done the photographs for the Gene catalogs."

photography with a professional who took private students.

Back in New York, Steven worked for a book producer/packager where he was involved with photographing a variety of subjects. For example, he traveled all over the country photographing collections for the *Time/Life* series the *Encyclopedia of Collectibles*. This was a time of hard training on all the technical aspects of photography, since he would set up a studio in the collectors' homes. He remembers the doll shoot in particular as one of his favorites.

He says he is not a collector, but does have a small collection of pottery from the 1920s through the 1940s. He also leans toward collecting photographs, especially black and white shots. Keith Carter is one photographer he admires because of the extraordinary animals he pictures. "They are so tender and moving, sometimes mysterious, but always evocative and beautiful."

Since he and Mel worked on the initial photographs of *Gene,* Steven has done the photographs for the *Gene* catalogs. Twice a year Joan Green comes to New York for the shoots and they, along with Mel, spend four or five days recording the new collection on film. He says that his studio "becomes a microcosm of 7th Avenue. There are miniscule shoes and handbags, and jewelry everywhere. We move props such as tiny columns in and out. And there is a table full of *Genes* waiting for their time on the runway." Sometimes, he says, the New York artists who designed the outfits drop by to observe and ooh and ahh.

The first time he worked on a *Gene*

shoot with Mel and Joan, Steven thought they were crazy. "They would say things like 'now she looks warm and friendly' or 'she looks too haughty.' But after a while I could look in the camera and see an attitude." He is amazed at the different kinds of moods you can get just by tweaking the angle of the head.

Photographing *Gene* isn't easy, according to Steven, mainly because of the technical problems. He admits that he uses every piece of lighting equipment in the studio "because she is small but has a tremendous amount of detail. Every bit of lighting is needed to pick out the different details – her hair, her jewelry, the sequins on her dress." It is an art to aim the lights in all the right spots, and to block them out in others so that the light doesn't spill over into the wrong place. He says that he almost breaks *Gene* down into parts for the lighting – the wrist, the hand, and so on, since each is a different problem. They spend two to three hours getting each shot ready.

The most challenging *Gene* shoot was the time he and his assistant were given 15 minutes apiece for a *Gene* shoot instead of the hours he was used to allowing for each shot in the studio. But, he explains, it was a different situation. They set up a studio in the Newark Airport to shoot the one-of-a-kind dolls that had been made for a convention. They were photographs just for a record, not the works of art he is used to providing.

Steven has never done fashion photography, but he likes to imagine that "the shoots are as full of joy, music, and laughter as the *Gene* shoots." He says they spin fantasies about *Gene's* life as they work. As an ex-English professor, he loves the creative writing aspect of working on the *Gene* Team. "It is a cool thing," he thinks, "that *Gene* is a character with a career, history, and fascinating personal life, and all of us that work on her get to contribute." *G*

Steven Mays has two favorite *Gene* dolls, "Monaco" which was the first one he shot and "Afternoon Off." "Afternoon Off is so simple and different. It reminds me of how the girls looked when I was in high school (in the 1960s). The cute girls wore sweaters and tight skirts."

"Savannah" was designed by student Katie McHale.

Young Designer of America Awards

In November of 1995, it was Joan Greene of Ashton-Drake who founded The Young Designer of America Competition. What has become an important program both to the *Gene* project, and to student participants across the country started in Santa Barbara, California. In late 1995, well-known curator, author and artist John Darcy Noble was invited to put on a doll exhibition at the Santa Barbara Museum of Art. Entitled "The Art of Play: Dolls and Toys Past and Present," the exhibit included 500 of the rarest and most spectacular dolls that could be amassed. Mel and Ashton-Drake felt especially honored when Mr. Noble chose *Gene* to represent the contemporary fashion doll.

While John Darcy Noble was concentrating on what was to be one of the most amazing doll exhibits ever, Mel went to work on recruiting such famous designers as his friend Geoffrey Beene to design and create one of a kind *Gene* dolls for the exhibit. There were six special designer *Gene* dolls created for the exhibit. Geoffrey Beene, William Ivey Long, Koos...., Timothy J. Alberts, Tim Kennedy and Doug James were the contributing designers. Two of the designs shown at the museum became the inspiration for dolls that were produced in the *Gene* Collection: "Bird of Paradise" and "Night at Versailles."

During this time, Joan Greene was working to find ways for the *Gene* exhibit to have more relevance in the community. Joan, along with Virginia Cochran from the public affairs office at the Santa Barbara Museum of Art and Kasia Stefanek the art teacher at Santa Barbara High School, began a series of discussions. Before long, Joan, who describes herself as a dreamer, offered to send 30-plus *Gene* dolls to Kasia's class.

When asked, both Mel and Joan say that they would have given almost anything to have had the opportunity in high school to design for a real company. It was Joan's idea to give the winners of the competition the opportunity to have their designs produced for the *Gene* Collection. What makes this competition so different and special is that those students who create designs that go into the *Gene* Collection receive royalties.

During the months from November 1995 until the first awards ceremony in May 1996, it was Joan and her assistant, Frank Rotundo who wrote letters to the students, scrounged for beautiful bits and pieces of fabric to send their way, and planned the details of the awards ceremony. Kasia remembers that Joan kept telling her that if they could make a difference to one student, the effort would be worth it.

Some of Joan's interest and enthusi-

LEFT:
Young designers Shelley Rinker and Michelle Guiterrez with Mel Odom and art teacher Kasia Stefanek.

Michelle Guiterrez with her design "The King's Daughter."

Shelly Rinker and her design for "Sparkling Seduction."

asm for the program comes from her first job out of college as a public school art teacher. She knows the difference that art can make to a student. She talks of art as being a way of living, but not necessarily as a way of making a living. Joan sees the Young Designer Program as an exercise in problem solving. "They start with a naked doll and a blank sheet of paper and if they stick with it, every student has the 'win' of seeing a completed design." She says that "they learn that art is about seeing, about believing in yourself, and taking the project through to the finish."

The program that stemmed from one product developer's dream and a dedicated teacher's hard work has made a difference in more than one student's life. It has expanded to several schools across the country. Each

Mel Odom and Abigail Haskell, the student who designed "Sunday Afternoon."

Katie McHale holds her winner "Savannah."

student who completes the program receives a certificate of completion, a special sterling silver pin designed by Greene, and winners receive cash prizes, as well as the possibility of actually seeing their design manufactered.

On an individual basis the program has changed lives. Santa Barbara student Shelley Rinker's design, "Sparkling Seduction" has become one of the top selling *Gene* dolls of all time and is the winner of *Gene*'s first doll award, the 1997 *Doll's* magazine Dolls of Excellence Award. With the help of the royalties and the confidence that Shelley has gained from the Young Designer program she is following her dream to attend college at Otis School of Design in California.

Shelley says that in the beginning she didn't realize that the designs were part of a contest, she just thought it was a school assignment. The teacher showed them old movies from *Gene*'s time and she came up with a design of a dress she would like to wear. She praises Joan "She is so amazing. She had this vision and made dreams come true for so many young designers."

Michele Gutierrez, another Santa Barbara student, designed "The King's Daughter" which became the first limited edition *Gene*. Michele will soon complete cosmotology school.

Another student winner, Mark Esposito, a junior at New York High School of Fashion Industries designed "Destiny" which became the first Annual Edition *Gene* doll. Winning has been a dream come true for Mark who for years has been designing dolls in his spare time. Esposito, who is severely hearing impaired, could not hear his name being called when it was announced that he had won. The message is now clear to him that he has talent and that his goal of attending the Fashion Institute of Technology is closer to reality. His royalties will help his dream come true.

The student competition is judged in the individual schools across the country. The judges always include art community leaders and Mel or a member of the design team. To date the judges have included John Darcy Noble, Mel Odom, Doug James, Timothy Alberts, Frank Rotundo, Larry Gordon, and Joan Greene.

Since 1997 the winners whose designs have been selected to go into the *Gene* Collection have been honored with a party at New York's famous Plaza Hotel. FAO Schwarz has hosted signings for Mel and the students during the 1997 and 1998 Toy Fairs.

Joan Green stated: "The Young Designer Program, in many ways, mirrors *Gene*'s success – girl dreams, girl works hard, and girl is discovered. All of us at Ashton-Drake are truly proud to sponsor this program that has successfully created a partnership between the arts, education, and business."

"I would have killed for this opportunity to have such a program when I was in school," Mel says. "The Young Designer Program has been Joan's baby from start to finish. The student's talent never ceases to amaze and delight me. I am so proud that *Gene* can inspire such creativity." *G*

ABOVE:
Scott Chambers for FAO Schwarz is presented the first "Sparkling Seduction" by Mel Odom and Shelley Rinker.

LEFT:
Mel and Joan Green with Mark Esposito the Young Designer of America Award winner who designed "Destiny."

New Designers for 1999

As the *Gene* phenomena has grown, more people have joined the team to accomplish what needs to be done to satisfy the star's growing public. The original 82nd Street Fashion Coalition were the pacesetters whose designs made *Gene* the best-dressed, best-coiféd doll, ever. Now, several new designers are scheduled to also contribute outfits for the 1999 *Gene* line.

The work of the new designers will be unveiled at the New York Toy Fair in February of 1999. Because of the timing of this book, the new designers are being introduced, but their creations are still a secret.

Jose Ferrand

In 1976, Jose came to the US to study at the Boston School of Fashion Design. Jose was introduced to the world of *Gene* at the Plaza event at the 1997 Toy Fair. A friend of photographer Steven May, he attended the party and "loved it."

Later he approached Mel at a signing and asked to be a *Gene* designer. Jose's background is in designing women's cocktail suits and dresses. He has worked for several well-recognized names on 7th Avenue.

A collector of vintage *Barbie*® dolls, Jose specialized in dolls prior to 1968. A native of Lima, Peru, he cites the political arena in Peru as the reason – around 1968 is

when the imports stopped. He is still interested in good quality vintage dolls, but says he was "buying dolls when they were $18. I like the *Barbie*® dolls of my childhood, but don't like redoing them."

The photograph of "Pin-Up" in a magazine appealed to Jose and he asked Steve May if there was a *Gene* catalog available. "Red Venus" was his first *Gene*, and he now owns five dolls and several costumes.

After the Plaza event, Jose started sewing his own creations for *Gene*. He feels that she is more satisfying to sew for than *Barbie*® because of her size. "*Gene* makes more of an impression – *Barbie*® is all hair!" he states.

"I love the 1940's and 50's movies that I watched as a child. I knew all the movie star's names, even in Peru," Jose says. "I was always interested in the movies, even the silent ones." He tells that "one Christmas my brother got a movie star book and I got an art book. His book became mine! I loved the glamorous pictures." After four years in Boston, he moved to New York City. He "paid his dues" by designing jeans, but then "got a break" on 7th Avenue. "Sometimes it is hard to break out of a mold. If you design jeans, only jeans companies are interested in you." He has worked for Oleg Cassini and others.

Jose says he likes doing both the prototype and pattern. "Sometimes a dress looks simple, but the construction is complicated." Jose admits to being a perfectionst. He likes to make certain that everything "is done in the right order. That can take preplanning, for example sometimes you can't get to the sleeves after the side seams have been sewn."

When he invited Mel over to see some clothes he had designed for *Gene*, he had four outfits and a group of sketches to show him of 40s and 50s era styles. He also likes clothes from the early 60s that are "so architectural." Jose works via fax and phone with Mel, talking about things such as "changing the color of a dress to make it look younger."

His criteria as a collector has always been to look at the doll first, then at the costume. "I go for the doll first, the outfits can change." He has a "Bird of Paradise" *Gene* dressed in a "Monaco" gown that "looks like Grace Kelly." He thinks the "Bird of Paradise" looks "more like New York or Paris, the others look more Hollywood." *G*

Vince Nowell

"If there is ever a story like *Gene Marshall's*, I'm living it," says Vince Nowell. "I started collecting *Gene* two years ago. I have been a *Barbie*® collector all my life and there was no way I'd collect another doll. Then I saw *Gene* at a doll show..." He belongs to a small *Gene* club in the Los

Angeles area, and admits "we're all severe *Gene* groupies!"

He wrote to Mel and said how much he loved the *Gene* doll and included his phone number. Mel called, and then later Vince met both Joan and Mel at a doll show. In these conversations, some of Vince's background emerged.

Vince was born and grew up in New Orleans, the baby of nine children. His mother was a dress designer who taught him to sew when he was 12 years old. His preference was always for making miniature clothes.

He moved to California eight years ago to attend design school and landed a job working for FAO Schwarz.

Vince began making clothes for *Gene* just "as a fan." But he has now created two outfits which have been definitely accepted for the 1999 line, and is working on a third one. "If ever something is fate and destiny, this is!"

Part of the draw to *Gene,* Vince thinks, "is the soap opera aspect. I can't wait to get the next doll, the next outfit. I'm so hooked on her biography." We can't wait to find out the next part of the story, he says, speaking for many fans. "I almost forget that she's not a real person."

Vince's message to *Gene* fans is "Thank you for supporting and loving this doll." He believes "the best is yet to come!" *G*

Christine DeNaile Curtis

Christine DeNaile Curtis is a professional artist who became a *Gene* designer as a result of doing a favor for her daughter.

Growing up in the New Jersey shore communities of Allanhurst and Diehl, and living as an adult in Bay Head and Bricktown, Christine attended the Traphagen School of Design and Illustration in New York City. After college she had several jobs relating to fashion: at Abraham Strauss, working at Vogue Patterns, and designing ballet costumes for a company in New Jersey. However, her favorite aspect of the arts was illustration, so most of her career has been doing a combination of commercial illustration and fine art, especially portraits and landscapes in pastels and watercolor. Her illustrations have appeared in numerous magazines and newspapers such as the *New York Times*.

Not a doll collector herself, she has a daughter who is a *Gene* collector. When her daughter attended the *Gene* convention last year, she asked her mother to design a costume for a doll. Christine dressed the *Gene* doll is a 50's style ball gown that would have been the kind of fashion seen on Grace Kelly – an opulent lavender gown with a long beaded and scalloped tunic. After seeing it, the *Gene* Team asked her if she would be interested in designing something for the 1999 *Gene* line.

She says she understands the attraction *Gene* has for her daughter who is a professional ballerina – the doll has long graceful limbs and looks like she could be a ballerina.

Christine is a writer as well as an artist. She has had children's stories published that are informative as well as entertaining, for example *Are Sharks Good for Anything?* And *This Fish Climbs Trees*. (Yes, Christine says the Mudskipper really does climb Mango trees.)

"Ideas come easily," says Christine, "I'm an artist!" Her inspiration comes "from a mixed bag," she even has many things she designed years ago that could be an inspiration for *Gene* costumes. Collectors have at least a couple of elegant ensembles from her to look forward to in the 1999 line, and Christine has lots more ideas! *G*

Lynne Day

Lynne Day is not only a doll collector,

her work is creating costumes for real-life movie stars. Who better to design clothing for *Gene*?

Lynne grew up in the San Francisco Bay area and attended San Francisco State University and earned a MFA at the University if Minnesota. She spent some time after college in the Midwest, working in Chicago and Minneapolis, and moved to the Los Angeles area 15 years ago. She has worked at several costume shops, and is currently with Bill Hargate Costumes.

Lynne says she is "tickled that *Gene* is in the film business. Films are such a cooperative effort with so many people behind the scenes.

In her job, Lynne gets to see all of the stock – the wonderful costumes from the 1940s. She admits that once in a while her work is mundane, such as the time they made bomb disposal suits for a movie. The real ones are so heavy that the actors couldn't wear them for the action sequences, so Lynne worked on recreating them in foam and canvas. "Being under a mountain of the things that outweighed me" isn't her favorite memory.

Lynne considers herself lucky to work on the peignoirs for Kim Bassinger for *LA Confidential* as well as her costumes in the first *Batman* movie. She made clothes for Angelica Huston for both *Addams Family* films. "I saw nothing but black for five solid months!" But she points out that the clothes are in six or seven shades of black! Lynne also worked on the clothes for Julia Roberts in *Pretty Woman*, including the famous red dress, and costumes for *Steel Magnolia, Thelma and Louise, The Truman Show,* and *Bugsy,* among others. She also made the costumes for a phone service commercial that starred 100 dogs in pants!

For the films, designers sketch the fashions and choose the fabrics, and then Lynne and her coworkers create the actual clothes. "We have to try and make the fabric look exactly like the sketch." There are many fittings on the actresses, "sometimes it is a mob scene with their nanny and children."

For a film they make multiples of each costume. Sometimes, too, they have to duplicate the actresses' outfits for stunt people or photo doubles.

Lynne is an avid "doll person." When she first saw an ad for *Gene* "I got the first one. I thought it can't be as good as it looks, but I opened the box and fell in love!" She loves the surprise when she opens the box with each new *Gene* or *Gene* outfit. "They are so exceptional in the detailing and finishing." She belongs to a doll group that gets together to play with *Gene.* "Her scale is so refreshing after 11-1/2 inches. You can incorporate so much detail."

"Our standard of taste in clothing today is so mundane and so boring," Lynne believes. "People under the age of 35 have only known minimalist clothing. In the 1940s and 50s clothing was playful and so specific. It is social history that people are discovering with *Gene.* At the turn of the century, soon the people from that era will be gone and this doll will be a reminder of that period of cultural history."

Lynne also likes that "sharing the dream" means that anyone can imagine a part of the *Gene* story by creating "your own movie – you can be *Gene's* agent, her costumer, her mom, her sister… the story frees the imagination rather than limiting it." She says that her *Gene* group often reminisce about how things would have been in *Gene's* day – topics like taking the red line trolley, or having zippers in swimsuits. "*Gene* sparks people to be interested in the past. Popular culture lasts only as long as people remember, or as it is preserved in movies."

Speaking of products that "have legs," Lynne feels that *Gene* is a product with such integrity, quality and consistent vision, that she "has great legs." A perfect description in more than one sense! *G*

Dolls & Costumes

Mel Odom, in an interview for a *New York Times* article, is quoted as saying "I was always fascinated with movie fashion… The clothes always looked so exotic to me, so sophisticated, so glamorous."

Gene's fashions are an integral part of her appeal. The costumes and the story line are linked in that each outfit increases the collector's knowledge of Gene's fictional biography. Every *Gene* doll and every *Gene* costume comes with a pamphlet that describes the movie scene or occasion in *Gene*'s private life when the ensemble was worn. The descriptions are very much in the style of the movie magazines of the period, as Mel put it "with a slightly naive slant like the magazines reported" in the days before private lives were dissected for the public. Each doll and each outfit increases the collector's knowledge of *Gene*'s fictional story line.

Ashton-Drake has also created collectors' cards with a color photograph of *Gene* on one side and information on the reverse describing the outfit and a short "movie review" quote about *Gene* wearing this ensemble. In this chapter, the "movie reviews" are quoted in italics, just as they appear on the Ashton-Drake cards. The

Gene is an amalgam of all the larger-than life actresses of Hollywood's Golden Era, a miniature mannequin for meticulously made clothes harking back to the glory days of Edith Head and Adrian

descriptions of each of the costumes are also direct from the collectors' cards. Whenever possible, a quote about the particular doll or outfit is included, either from Mel Odom, Joan Greene, one of the designers, or other *Gene* experts. They often point out the differences between the original prototype design and the factory manufactured final garment.

Mel points out that "*Gene* is a very contemporary take on that period. You cannot create (an outfit) to look like it's from that period completely, because if you look at movie star dolls of that period. The Deanna Durbin dolls for example, they were basically children's bodies and faces sometimes dressed up in adult's clothes. They were not this body that *Gene* has, and that sophisticated face that *Gene* has, even if it is supposed to be that star back then. It's still a child's version of that star's face. And I'm glad for *Gene* to be a contemporary take on that period."

Frank DeCaro, in a *New York Times* article in February 1998, observed that *Gene*, "taller than *Barbie*®" and infinitely better dressed" is "an amalgam of all the larger-than life actresses of Hollywood's Golden Era, a miniature mannequin for meticulously made clothes harking back to the glory days of

Edith Head and Adrian."

Collectors are fascinated with the quality and fine detail of the *Gene* clothing. The whole approach from Mel, the designers and Ashton-Drake has been to create miniature versions of real clothes – clothes that can be removed and handled and with snaps and buttons that work. As Mel puts it, "Our philosophy has been we don't do doll clothes, we do people clothes on doll scale." He goes on to explain "That is what *Barbie*® had early on, her clothes were real clothes, identifiable clothes. I think that is a very seductive thing. I know how I'm a sucker for miniature of practically anything. And we've had people collect *Gene* who don't even collect dolls. He relates that a number of people have told him "I've never bought a doll in my life, but the details on these clothes are so wonderful." Others have told him it is like owning a piece of the *Theatre de la Mode*.

One of the designers, Tim Kennedy has said "*Gene*'s clothes could not look like doll clothes. There is very little compromise in the detail and the cut of her clothes. The linings are very complicated to do, for example, they are not easy to manufacture or less expensive to produce."

The costumes are successful on an esthetic level, but they also are highly popular with the people who buy them because they can be "played with" and handled. As Sonia Rivera, Editor of *Gene Scene* says, "When I got my doll, ordered from that first ad for *Gene*, right away I had her out of the box and her clothes changed." The extra details, the jewelry and other tiny accessories, beg to be handled and tried on the dolls. How can a collector resist?

As Tim Kennedy puts it: "People yearn for a time more optomistic, more romantic, more beautiful and glamorous, more magic as the times of the 1940s appear to be. We don't see the clothes and grooming in movies any more (like it was in the 40s). People wouldn't dare to wear *Gene's* clothes,

but they don't have the reservations with her wearing them that they would have if they wore the clothes themselves." He goes on to say that "it all has to do with self image. Ours may be fragile and we wear things that are safe and accepted. *Gene* can wear anything and it doesn't infringe on a person's acceptance. People (in their own lives) don't necessarily understand, accept or buy the most brilliant designs to wear since clothing is very much security and they wear what is acceptable in their social circle. But to Hollywood stars, Armani is a necessity!"

The 1995 Line

The first direct mail campaign in 1995 consisted of a 12-page catalog showing three dolls and nine outfits. The promotional letter that was mailed with it announced: "Close your eyes. A dream is about to come true." The catalog reads "As carefully chosen as her dramatic roles, her wardrobe was the envy of all…From the Hamptons to Hollywood, she looked stunning wherever she appeared."

"Premiere"

1995
Designed by Tim Kennedy
Item #96401 (includes doll)
Retired 9/96
Original price $69.95
From card:

"Would you know a new star if you saw one? Ask hundreds of fans who flocked outside Monolithic Studio's latest film premiere of 'Blonde Lace.' Fans were dazzled by the up-and-coming new star Gene Marshall – the studio's hottest new property. Miss Marshall turned all heads in a gown of black velvet and burnished gold. In this film she stepped into a starring role at the last moment...and her performance has all of Hollywood buzzing. This is a new face and talent to reckon with."

"Premiere" is a two-piece evening gown created for the limelight! The velvet jacket is cut straight off the shoulder and fully lined with patterned gold lamé. The breathtaking skirt is black lace over antique gold taffeta, shimmering with hundreds of hand-applied beads and sequins, and hemmed in black velvet. "Premier" is circa 1941, and was designed exclusively for Gene by Tim Kennedy.

Mel Odom: "The original prototype of "Premier" was done in red and lavender. But "Red Venus" was happening and that was already definitely red, so the colors were changed."

This was the first doll to be retired by Ashton-Drake. Even though it was introduced at the same time as "Red Venus" and "Monaco," the story line indicated that this was the first gown worn by the young starlet.

"Monaco"

1995
Designed by Timothy Alberts
Item #96403 (doll included)
Retired
Original price $69.95
From card:

"The fairy-tale comes true for Gene Marshall in 'Monaco,' her newest film for Monolithic Studios. She plays a girl of common birth who wins the heart of her nation's handsome prince. Her wedding scene is the dreamiest on film yet...but we can't say more! Our guess? A host of filmstruck 1950 brides will be trying their best to duplicate this look for themselves."

"Monaco" is a fabulous bridal ensemble, much imitated in its time. The gown has a bodice of lace over satin with collar, cuffs and bowed belt of satin. The skirt is a confection of layered tulle with hand-fashioned ribbon roses, and a separate tie-on net slip. With "pearl"-trimmed headpiece and veil, bridal bouquet, matching shoes, seamed hose and jewelry. "Monaco" is circa 1950, and was designed exclusively for *Gene* by Timothy Alberts.

Timothy Alberts: " Monaco is my favorite of my designs for *Gene*." It was originally made for the plaster prototype doll. The bodice was made from a piece of antique lace and the roses were larger. The headpiece had a big bow in the back and was based on a Russian Court headdress.

"Red Venus"
1995
Designed by Tim Kennedy
Item #96402 (includes doll)
Original price $69.95
From card:

"Film fans of Gene Marshall: get ready for this! It's 'Red Venus,' her first 'bad-girl' role, and furthermore, her first screen appearance as a ravishing redhead. She plays a gangster's moll with a story to hide…but her on-screen gowns do plenty of revealing, in that sly, sexy way that studio designers know so well. The climactic final scene will have you hating her character, envying her figure…and cheering her electrifying performance!"

"Red Venus" is the perfect gown for a gangster's paramour: ruby taffeta, off-the-shoulder, with dramatic asymmetrical draping across the hips. With a sensational boa of gathered tulle layered in two colors; let *Gene* hold it above her head or sling it impetuously to the ground! With matching shoes, hose and jewelry. "Red Venus" is circa 1944, and was designed exclusively for *Gene* by Tim Kennedy.

Mel Odom: "People love "Red Venus" because she has long hair. I had companies say 'Don't even send us a red-haired doll, we can't sell it.' And she was our best seller in the first group. I had always drawn a lot of redheads, they had been sort of my specialty. And I knew I was going to do *Gene* as a red-head, but there was literally a stigma against redhead dolls."

Joan Greene: "In 1994 Tim Kennedy sent this wonderful dress, done like a high-couture draped dress, "Red Venus". Usually for people this kind of draping is done as one-of-a-kind dress by someone like Oscar de la Renta. It became a nightmare to do it for a doll. I sent it out to seamstresses to duplicate and they couldn't get it. The pattern looked like it couldn't possibly be a dress. I was nervous about it, thinking 'What am I going to do?' So I decided to color code it so we could show what matched what. After color coding the pattern a messenger took it to a seamstress and within two hours she had made the first dress. So we sent the color coded pattern to the factory."

"Blond Lace"
1995
Designed by Tim Kennedy
Item #96404 (costume only)
Retired 6/1/98
Original price $29.95
From card:

"A new face has caught the light that only stars reflect...a rare light indeed. It shines on a young actress named Gene Marshall. She's the good-hearted cigarette girl in 'Blond Lace,' director Eric Von Sternberg's newest film from Monolithic. This once small role was reworked at the 11th hour when the original star suffered an injury. Miss Marshall, dressed in the most feminine of tuxedos, does a dance number on the film's nightclub stage with an easy grace, and a few breathy words guaranteed to break hearts from here to Poughkeepsie!"

"Blond Lace" is a chic tuxedo with tailored jacket, slacks and lace-trimmed halter top. Lace cuffs, a black velvet beret and a tiny boutonniere completes the ensemble. With matching shoes, hose and a "pearl"-topped cane. "Blond Lace" is circa 1941, and was designed exclusively for *Gene* by Tim Kennedy.

"Pink Lightning"
1995
Designed by Tim Kennedy
Item #96405 (costume only)
Retired 6/1/98
Original price $29.95
From card:

"In a gala reception last Thursday, studio head Rubin Lilienthal announced Monolithic's first Gene Marshall musical, titled 'Bird of Paradise,' due for Spring release. Miss Marshall charmed us with an impromptu rendition of 'There's a Small Hotel' sung at the piano. She was dazzling as ever, in blue taffeta with a dramatic zig-zag hem of pink and silver. We're told Miss Marshall agreed to the musical project only if she could do her own film dubbing – no problem there!"

"Pink Lightning" is true Hollywood dazzle: midnight blue taffeta with a portrait neckline, set off by shocking pink organdy draped at the bosom and around the shoulders. A flash of pink and silver lamé defines the unique staggered hemline. With matching shoes and clutch handbag. "Pink Lightning" is circa 1956, and was designed exclusively for *Gene* by Tim Kennedy.

"Striking Gold"
     1995
     Designed by Timothy Alberts
     Item #96407 (costume only)
     Retired 6/1/98
     Original price $29.95
     From card:

"One of the surprise recipients of the Golden Star awards last night was actress Gene Marshall, winner of the Best Actress award for her role in 'The Black Ribbon.' We say 'surprise' only because it's a real Tinseltown rarity for an actress only two years into her Hollywood career, and barely 20, to win such kudos from the industry and public alike. But Miss Marshall's graciousness and poise, as she accepted the award in a gown as glittering and golden as her statuette, hint at even greater awards to come."

"Striking Gold" is a golden sheath with a halter neckline, accented with rhinestones at the bustline. With matching golden knit gloves, and a tassled, beaded stole in pale chartreuse and shell pink. *Gene* also wears "golden star" jewelry to celebrate her award. "Striking Gold" is circa 1943, and was designed exclusively for *Gene* by Timothy Alberts.

Mel Odom: "Once in awhile there are technical problems in making an outfit. On "Striking Gold" the factory didn't get the stole right until it was at the end of production."

"Usherette"
     1995
     Designed by Tim Kennedy
     Item #96408 (costume only)
     Original price $29.95
     From card:

"In Hollywood lore it's known that in Gene Marshall's first publicity photos, she wears an usherette uniform. It seems that when director Eric Von Sternberg attended the 1941 premiere of his film 'Manhattan Nights,' Miss Marshall was the usherette who showed him to his seat. Taken with her unusual beauty, the producer used Gene's own flashlight to illuminate her lovely, photogenic face. Then they returned to the lobby, where he announced his 'discovery' to reporters amid the pop of flashbulbs."

"Usherette" is a jaunty four-piece uniform of velveteen piped with satin and accented with "pearls." It comes complete with jacket, short "tap pants," matching velveteen long pants, and a tasseled pillbox hat. Plus hose, shoes…and even a tiny flashlight! "Usherette" is circa 1941, and was designed exclusively for *Gene* by Tim Kennedy.

"Blue Evening"
    1995
    Designed by Timothy Alberts
    Item #96409 (costume only)
    Original price $29.95
    From card:

"Nothing seems to go together better than a beautiful woman and the songs about love that are inspired by them. But here's a twist on that tale! Actress Gene Marshall, ever the dress designers' darling, has inspired a gorgeous gown based on the song 'Blue Evening,' that moody, bluesy tune recorded by Ina Stafford. Gene Marshall is so fond of the gown – in deep blue satin by her top studio designer Timothy Alberts – that you'll see it in her latest publicity stills from Monolithic Studios this fall."

"Blue Evening" is a twilight-blue satin strapless gown with accents of deep rose at the draped bosom, and its own separate pink net slip. Includes rhinestone pin, "pearl" earrings, pink chiffon stole. Beaded choker, hose and matching shoes. "Blue Evening" is circa 1953, and was designed exclusively for *Gene* by Timothy Alberts.

"Love's Ghost"
    1995
    Designed by Doug James
    Item #96406 (costume only)
    Original price $29.95
    From card:

"In Gene Marshall's most unique film romance, 'Love's Ghost,' she plays a lovely guardian of two children in a Victorian setting. Set in a brooding period mansion, the film allows Miss Marshall to explore the question: 'Can a beautiful Victorian governess find eternal happiness with a restless spirit?' Many filmgoers are debating the true meaning of the film's conclusion. See it for yourself and be the judge...but be warned: take along a hanky!"

"Love's Ghost" is the essence of Victorian elegance. Blouse is of white lawn with deeply-ruffled neckline and lace edging, and fastens with hooks and eyes down the front. Matching skirt has a separate net slip. A flowered cummerbund and matching straw hat add color. With hose, white shoes, "pearl" earrings, and hair ribbon. "Love's Ghost" is circa 1946, and was designed exclusively for *Gene* by Doug James.

"The Kiss"
> **1995**
> **Designed by Tim Kennedy**
> **Item # 96410 (costume only)**
> **Original price $29.95**
> **From card:**

"I'll remember the end of this film as long as I live. There was Gene Marshall, 'slipping into something more comfortable' before sharing a romantic moment with her on-screen husband, as the two held each other in their arms, looking out over the twinkling lights of the Manhattan skyline. Then he kissed her, tenderly, yet so passionately... and the credits started to roll as the scene faded to black. It was the end of the movie, but not for me. That perfect kiss went on and on, even as I walked out of the theatre in perfect bliss."

"The Kiss" invites romance with a marabou-trimmed pink satin peignoir lined in shimmering silver lamé. Also included is a matching gown with "diamond" pin, earrings, and high-heeled mules. "The Kiss" is circa 1946, and was designed exclusively for *Gene* by Tim Kennedy.

Joan Greene: "I love the premise of 'The Kiss'. The old movies didn't have the graphic scenes like the ones today. There was a kiss at the end of the movie that gave it that sense of romance."

"Crimson Sun"
> **1995**
> **Designed by Doug James**
> **Item #93502 (costume only)**
> **Original price $29.95**
> **From card:**

This Hollywood reporter sat in at the recent studio session where Gene Marshall was being photographed for her first wartime pin-up. It went like this: 'All right, Miss Marshall, let's have a little more leg for those boys in uniform. Now let's get that windblown look in the hair...walk toward me...fabulous! Now let's make it sweet, but smoldering. Remind them of the girl back home. Love in the eyes...wish you were here...perfect!' And if you've seen the results, folks, you know it IS perfect."

"Crimson Sun" is an ingenious one-piece halter-top knot swimsuit with the look of a two-piece. Ensemble includes floral-print sarong, matching hat, fabric-trimmed beach tote, and golden, ankle-wrap sandals with matching belt...plus golden earrings and a matching bracelet! "Crimson Sun" is circa 1943, and was designed exclusively for *Gene* by Doug James.

"Good-Bye New York"
    1995
    Designed by Doug James
    Item #93501 (costume only)
    Original price $29.95
    From card:

"Lucky travelers at Grand Central got a major eyeful last Tuesday if they happened to be heading toward Track 14. Noted Hollywood producer Eric Von Sternberg was off to the City of Dreams…and at his side, a young lady named Gene Marshall, his latest and most luscious discovery, a dynamite blonde in a fur-trimmed suit."

"Good-Bye New York" is a two-piece suit in crepe and tweed with "fur" accents, worn with a jersey blouse. Complete with matching "fur" hat and muff, which has a tiny pocket for her hanky in the back. Jewelry includes golden teardrop earrings and a heart-shaped scatter pin with chain., shoes, seamed hose, hat box and even *Gene*'s childhood teddy bear, fully jointed, to keep her company! Fabrics may vary. "Good-Bye New York" is circa 1941, and was designed exclusively for *Gene* by Doug James.

Mel Odom: "We didn't have a clue in the beginning that the level of manufacturing would be high enough that we could line these garments. We didn't know how high to aim. The prototype of "Good-Bye New York" that we sent (to the Phillippines) was lined, and when it came back from the factory it was lined."

Joan Greene: "My personal favorite costume is "Good-Bye New York" because it has not only the costume, but her hat box and teddy bear. I feel close to that one, Mel sent a clown for her to be carrying. I thought she had to have a teddy bear, so I called a friend, Debbie Ortega to make a bear for *Gene* instead."

The 1996 Line

"Pin-Up"
>**1996**
>**Designed by Tim Kennedy**
>**Item #93507 (includes doll)**
>**Original price $69.95**
>**From card:**

"After the impact of Gene Marshall's first pin-up for the war effort, 'Crimson Sun,' the G.I.s demanded 'give us more!' Now Monolithic Studios has done just that with this all-new pin-up poster. And it certainly gives the troops a lot more of Miss Marshall! She appears in a sizzling black teddy and matching negligee that should get every G.I.'s immediate attention. We can already hear the wolf whistles all the way from Corregidor to the coast of France!"

"Pin-Up" is *Gene*'s "gift" to the troops! Black-laced satin teddy is accented with pink ribbon, including ribbon lacing up the back. Complete with matching lace-trimmed negligee and laced heels. No wonder the G.I.s loved it! "Pin-Up" is circa 1944, and was designed exclusively for *Gene* by Tim Kennedy.

Mel Odom: " "Pin-Up" was one of the six prototype costumes which Mel took to Ashton-Drake initially. "Pin-Up" was one of the very first things we showed them, and it went into the second line."

"Blue Goddess"
>**1996**
>**Designed by Tim Kennedy**
>**Item #93503 (includes doll)**
>**Retired**
>**Original price $69.95**
>**From card:**

"Hot news in Hollywood this month: the color of Gene Marshall's eyes! In 'Blue Goddess,' the camera just can't seem to tear itself away from her mesmerizing baby-blues...unless it's to reveal her knockout figure in a gown that was designed to match those eyes to a T! 'Blue Goddess' may be the stolen gem that gives this film its title, but it's Gene who deserves the title of 'goddess' here!"

"Blue Goddess" is a strapless gown in aqua chiffon with an attached stole, beautifully draped to highlight *Gene*'s figure, and accented by a hint of hand beading. The stole can be worn over the head, draped across the back or around the shoulders. Complete with matching shoes, hose, an aqua necklace, drop "diamond" earrings and a rhinestone and aqua bracelet. "Blue Goddess" is circa 1945, and was designed exclusively for *Gene* by Tim Kennedy.

Mel Odom: "A man came up to me at the convention holding a "Blue Goddess," and said, 'I want you to know this is what I have of my mother now. She died two months ago and this looks just like she did when she was young. She was really beautiful.' When you hear people place something you've created in such a personal place in their life, you feel like you've really hit the bone of that individual."

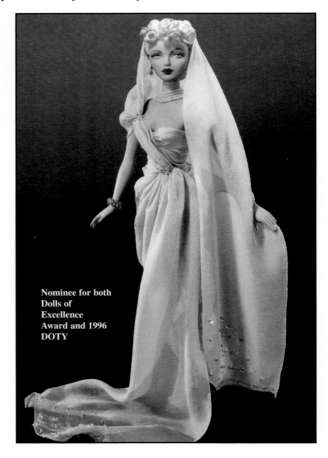

Nominee for both Dolls of Excellence Award and 1996 DOTY

"Crescendo"
    1996
    Designed by Doug James
    Item #93505 (costume only)
    Original price $39.95
    From card:

"In 'Crescendo,' Gene Marshall enacts one of the most dramatic stories of her career. She is a young American violinist forced to end her overseas musical studies and flee Europe – and a passionate love affair – in 1939. Years later she returns to Europe as an established concert artist. And in the midst of performing, she sees her former lover, thought to have perished, in the audience before her. The power and emotion of Miss Marshall's performance in that scene alone is truly award-inspiring."

"Crescendo" is a striking gown of deep emerald taffeta with a separate fuchsia underskirt, fuchsia crystal buttons and a white lace bodice that is hand-beaded. Includes a miniature violin, sheet music, and matching hose, shoes, jewelry and hanky. "Crescendo" is circa 1946, and was designed exclusively for *Gene* by Doug James.

Mel Odom: "I think "Crescendo" is one of the most astonishing things we have ever created. It is so complex: the lace is beaded, the cartridge pleats in the back – we never would have done it the first year, because it is just too complicated. In fact, when we shipped it off (to the factory) I was thinking, 'Well, these pleats will be gone in the back, and probably the beading on the bodice will be gone." The manufactured version "came back exactly as we sent it."

Doug James: "I translated a neckline Mel had seen into something suitable for *Gene*. I suggested that *Gene* should be carrying a sheet of music if she were a violinist. Mel agreed but said the music had to be *Humoresque*."

"El Morocco"
    1996
    Designed by Timothy Alberts
    Item #93506
    Original price $29.95
    From card:
"It's not an easy trip from the big screen to the smaller one, but actress <u>Gene Marshall</u> made it seem that way in her first TV interview. Viewed on NBS last Saturday at 7:00, Miss Marshall was a gracious hostess in her parents' home. And stunning, too, in a cocktail dress of satin and tulle, worn with diamond scatter pins. Later, the Marshalls were seen at El Morocco, out to celebrate <u>Dr. Edward Marshall's</u> 60th birthday."

"El Morocco" is a deep plum taffeta sheath with a separate overskirt of black tulle, jet buttons and a black velvet bow at the waist. Includes a chic matching hat embellished with silk flowers, feathers, handbag, "diamond" scatter pins, bracelet, hose and shoes. "El Morocco" is circa 1955, and was designed exclusively for *Gene* by Timothy Alberts.

"Holiday Magic"
    1996
    Designed by Tim Kennedy
    Item #94392 (costume only)
    1st Limited and exclusive *Gene* item
        Dealer Exclusive,
        limited production of 2,000
    Original price $44.95
    From card:
"Actress Gene Marshall made one of her rare television appearances last evening on the fabulous 'Holiday Magic' special on NBS, one of the first shows in living color! Those lucky few with color sets got to see Gene in her shimmering blue-and-white gown, elegantly designed to match the white, blue and silver studio set. But even in black-and-white, she was something to see!"

"Holiday Magic" is a short evening gown with a bodice of cobalt satin and a frothy, full skirt of snow-white tulle. Blue satin bows cascade down the front of the skirt, and blue satin rosettes accent the back of the waist. Includes elbow-length white gloves, glittering jewelry, hose, matching shoes, and a tiny silver-and-blue gift-wrapped package. "Holiday Magic" is circa 1956, and was designed exclusively for *Gene* by Tim Kennedy.

"Holiday Magic" was inspired by Joan Greene's love of a dress that Grace Kelly wore. Joan sent the illustration to Tim Kennedy to translate for this first *Gene* exclusive.

"Afternoon Off"
      1996
      Designed by Doug James
      Item #93508 (costume only)
      Retired 6/1/98
      Original price $29.95
      From card:
"What does a Hollywood star do on her day off? Actress Gene Marshall tries to read as much of her fan mail as possible, as well as the magazine articles currently written about her. Miss Marshall recently delighted a fan by answering her letter with an authographed copy of 'Screen Look,' the current issue with the star on the cover. The magazine was inscribed: 'To Nancy, because you made me what I am today. Fondly, Gene.'"

"Afternoon Off" is a casual ensemble of a grey twill jacket lined in royal blue, tweed skirt, and a sweater with beaded trim at the neckline. Includes grey shoes, matching hose and a miniature copy of *Screen Look*, a classic movie fan magazine with a cover illustration of *Gene* by Mel Odom himself. Fabrics may vary. "Afternoon Off" is circa 1947, and was designed exclusively for *Gene* by Doug James.

Mel Odom: "I like for *Gene* to have a personal life because that gives her public life more of a resonance. "Afternoon Off" is one of my favorite costumes because it's about that – of her not working." The year that "Afternoon Off" came out at Toy Fair Mel says "one day I had five people tell me either they wore (an outfit like)that or their mother wore that. I recognized that people's memories are part of things – it's that connection with what they already have."

"Personal Secretary"
      1996
      Designed by Tim Kennedy
      Item #93542 (costume only)
      Original price $34.95
      From card:
"What career gal wouldn't be thrilled to step into Gene Marshall's shoes, especially those trim little backless heels she wears in her new comedy, 'Personal Secretary'? Gene's stylish, she's smart, and she takes such good care of her demanding ad-exec boss that he finds her indispensable. But when Gene brings him lunch from the Automat, a shared slice of banana cream pie leads to unexpected romance. Don't miss this one!"

"Personal Secretary" is a pert career ensemble of matte gray taffeta with a wide collar of crisp white organdy, matching cuffs, and white buttons in a "V" detail on the bodice. The hat and drawstring handbag are ingeniously crafted of chenille "violets" complete with tiny green leaves. Complete with hose and white shoes. "Personal Secretary" is circa 1957, and was designed exclusively for *Gene* by Tim Kennedy.

The 1997 Line

"Sparkling Seduction"
1997
Designed by Shelley Rinker
Item #94394 (includes doll)
Original price $79.95
From card:
"Fans of Gene Marshall will be dazzled by her performance in the new film 'Sparkling Seduction.' You'll be intrigued by her role as a chic, savvy private eye. And who else but Miss Marshall could make an entrance in a glittering gown that clings to every curve, arms swathed with fur, bedecked in jewels, and utter a line like 'What were you expecting, darling? A trench coat?'"

"Sparkling Seduction" is a strapless black gown with a furled hemline, glittering with applied pailettes. Worn with its full-length cape of claret velvet with sleeves of faux fur. An intricately beaded "amethyst" necklace, three-strand bracelet and earrings complete the ensemble. "Sparkling Seduction" is circa 1948, and was designed exclusively for *Gene* by Shelley Rinker, Winner of the 1996 Young Designers of America Award for "Best Period Costume."

"Iced Coffee"
1997
Designed by Laura Meisner
Item #94396 (includes doll)
Original price $79.95
From card:
"'My baby makes me nervous...like iced coffee. My baby is a habit that's hard to break.' Fans of Gene Marshall will thrill to her introduction of this jazzy nightclub number in her latest film for Monolithic. And to top it off, she sings this sexy lyric in a knockout gown, an eye-popping combination of chiffon and satin. This dress surely does show off Miss Marshall's major assets with sass, class and just the right touch of sparkle."

"Iced Coffee" is a gown with a shaped, gaithered bodice of café-au-lait chiffon worn above a slim column of creamy satin. The bodice extends into a swagged sash, fastened at the hip with a rhinestone pin. With glittering "diamond" jewelry, plus white evening gloves, hose and matching shoes. "Iced Coffee" is circa 1946, and was designed exclusively for *Gene* by Laura Meisner.

Mel Odom: "I think that the dress that "Iced Coffee" is wearing makes you think how beautiful *Gene* looks, not 'Isn't that a gorgeous dress,' but 'doesn't she look beautiful in that dress?' I love the snood on the hair, it's an almost foolproof way of getting the hair right."

"White Hyacinth"
    1997
    Designed by Doug James
    Item #94395 (includes doll)
    Original price $79.95
    Retired 6/1/98
    From card:

"Dear Miss Marshall: Enclosed for your consideration is a script titled 'White Hyacinth.' It's a compelling story about a couple who are deeply in love but can't stay together without creating havoc in their marriage. But you'll see that they work out their differences in a series of very moving and dramatic scenes. The final scene on a spring afternoon when the two reconcile is a show-stopper! We just can't imagine anyone other than you in this role, and sincerely hope you will accept it."

"White Hyacinth" is an ivory coat dress with sophisticated princess tailoring, sashed at the waist. It is worn over a peach-colored chemise slip. The matching hat features braided trim and felt accents. With clutch handbag, yellow gloves, shoes, hose and even a tiny "orchid" corsage. "White Hyancinth" is circa 1946, and was designed exclusively for *Gene* by Doug James.

"Bird of Paradise"
        1997
        Designed by William Ivey Long
        Item #94397 (includes doll)
        Original price $79.95
        From card:

"The scene opens in total darkness. Then a small spot of light appears. The eye can just make out a woman's figure, slowly descending a large staircase. As the spotlight widens, a thousand dazzling points of light flash from her graceful body. And as the light comes up, you realize it's Gene Marshall, swathed in crystalline splendor from head to toe, a vision you'll never forget!"

"Bird of Paradise" is the ultimate showgirl's ensemble. It features elaborate crystal beading over a bodysuit of flesh-toned net. Triple beaded swags from the hips are highlighted by accents of gathered, pale pink tulle. The feathered turban is of lavender iridescent fabric festooned with crystal drops. With matching spangled hose and shoes. "Bird of Paradise" is circa 1949, and was designed exclusively for Gene by William Ivey Long.

Mel Odom: " William Ivey Long is from North Carolina. He designs for Broadway and film. I met him when I went with friends to a President's Day party at the Chelsea Hotel. He came up to me and said 'I hear you can draw. Draw a mural of George Washington and some Valentines.' Twenty years later I asked him to design a one-of-a-kind Showgirl outfit for *Gene*. It was in the Santa Barbara Museum show. I reminded him 'You owe me for the mural!' The original one-of-a-kind costume had plumes rather than tulle in the back."

"Promenade"
1997
Designed by Tim Kennedy
Item #93541 (costume only)
Original price $29.95
Retired 6/1/98
From card:

"Gloria, isn't that Gene Marshall across the street, walking her dogs? Can you believe that fabulous suit she's wearing...and what a figure! Do you think she'd mind if we stopped to pet the dogs and asked for her autograph? I've heard she's very. Very nice."

"Promenade" is an orchid suit accented with navy-and-white gingham. The sleeveless blouse is worn under the fully-lined jacket. The fitted trumpet skirt has a flared hemline. With matching fabric shoes, veiled hat, gloves, and hose. "Promenade" is circa 1945, and was designed exclusively for *Gene* by Tim Kennedy.

"The King's Daughter"
1st Limited Edition Gene Doll –
Edition of 5,000
1997
Designed by Michele Guiterrez
Item #93525
Original price $99.95
From card:

"For our radio audience, here's a sample from Gene Marshall's newest film hit, 'The King's Daughter': 'Palace Life is so stifling, Edward. Father forbids it, but I must find a way to get out! I want to see what the world is like, not just looking down from this tower...but there in the streets, where the people live their lives with energy, wit and passion! Can you help me?'
'Yes, your Highness. I will come for you at midnight.'"

"The King's Daughter" is an 18th-century-inspired costume for *Gene*'s starring role in the movie of the same name. The overdress is of rich, royal-blue velvet embellished with lace and golden braided trim. It is worn over a lilac silk underskirt enhanced with delicate hand beading. Complete with tiara, "The King's daughter" was designed exclusively for *Gene* by Michele Guiterrez, Winner of the first Young Designers of America Award for "Best Overall Costume."

"Blossoms in the Snow"
1997 Retailer Exclusive,
limited production of 5,000
Designed by Tim Kennedy
Item #93544 (Costume only)
Original price $44.95
From card:

"Actress Gene Marshall was a standout among the glittering guests at the War Veteran's New Year's Eve charity ball, held last night on the stage of New York's Raleigh Theatre. Reflecting the event's theme of 'Blossoms in the Snow,' Miss Marshall wore a simple but stunning gown of pink satin, accented with white fur sprinkled with silken rose blossoms. She was a breath of fashion freshness among the evening's more conventional couture."

"Blossoms in the Snow" is a sophisticated gown in pink satin with rhinestone trim. Accents of white "fur" frame the shoulders, scattered with white satin rose blossoms. A matching muff, also trimmed with roses, adds particular elegance. Includes a lace-trimmed hanky, jewelry, hose, and matching shoes. "Blossoms in the Snow" is circa 1953, and was designed exclusively for *Gene* by Tim Kennedy.

Mandarin Mood"
1997
Designed by Tim Kennedy
Item #93543 (costume only)
Original price $34.95
From card:

"The most coveted dinner-party invitations in Hollywood are coming from the lovely Gene Marshall, who is known not only for the quality of the cuisine served in her home, but also for the unique and clever after-dinner entertainment she devises for her guests. At a recent party with an Oriental theme, the dragonboat races held in the star's swimming pool were the high spot of the evening."

"Mandarin Mood" lets *Gene* "dress the part" for her dinner party *extraordinaire*. She wears Chinese pajamas that feature a figured silk jacket, flared beneath the waist, and wide pants. The ensemble is piped in navy satin and the jacket features authentic frog closures. Complete with "coin" earrings, tiny chopsticks to be worn in her hair, and golden sandals. "Mandarin Mood" is circa 1946 and was designed exclusively for *Gene* by Tim Kennedy.

"Sea Spree"
    1997
    Designed by Tim Kennedy
    Item #93546 (costume only)
    Original price $34.95
    From card:

"Gene Marshall comes off as quite a plucky little lady in this live-ly new film, especially in this scene: 'Well, Ensign Richards, I can dance, all right! In fact, if I thought it would bring my Bobby back from the Pacific any sooner, I'd dance from here to President Roosevelt's front door, just to tell him how much I miss my fella. I'd dance across the decks of the whole 7th Fleet, just to find my man and throw my arms around him. Can I dance? Well, if it's for my man and all the others just like him, far from home and missin' their gals…you bet *I can dance!"*

"Sea Spree" is a crisp nautical number featuring a middy halter top with sailor collar, matching wide-legged pants with nautical button detailing, and loose-fitting jacket. Matching shoes, hose, jewelry and hair ribbon. "Sea Spree" is circa 1943 and was designed exclusively for *Gene* by Tim Kennedy.

"Tango"
    1997
    Designed by Tim Kennedy
    Item #93545 (costume only)
    Original price $39.95
    From card:

"Her gaze was fixed intently on his face, her body held so close-ly that the two dancers melted into one sinuous curve. I remember a flash of gold, a blur of blazing coral as Gene danced across the screen in his arms. And then suddenly he released her, so quickly that she seemed to spin away, out of control. But at the last moment, his muscular hand reached out to catch her wrist, and he slowly pulled her toward his body again. I gasped with the thrill of it all. So this was the tango!"

"Tango" is the ultimate dancer's dress; it suggests movement even when perfectly still. It is tailored of multi-layered coral chiffon with exotic beaded accents at the draped bosom, and a dramatic attached stole. With matching shoes, hose, golden bracelet and gypsy hoop earrings. Circa 1951. Designed by Tim Kennedy for the *Gene Marshall Collection.*

Mel Odom: "I will take a designer to a movie and will show them (an idea). I'll say 'let's do something based on that silhouette,' or ' let's do something with that neckline.' The costume "Tango's" neckline was from an Ava Gardner movie. The neckline, the way it formed an upside down heart was so beautiful – it focused all your attention on the face. The rest of it, the coral color, the eight symmetrical hemlines, all of that was Timmy's idea. Ava Gardner's dress was yellow with flowers on the bust. Timmy Kennedy said to me, 'This is going to be a big success, because everybody from the palest white woman to the darkest skinned black woman looks great in this coral color' and I think it has been our most successful costume to date."

"Midnight Romance"
    1997 PARKWEST/NALED
      Catalog Exclusive
    Designed by Timothy Alberts
    Item #93550 (includes doll)
    Original Price $89.95
    From card:

"Composer Johnny Harmon's newest recording, featuring his hit song 'Midnight Romance,' has an album cover that will stop you in your tracks! It features a gorgeous photo of none other than Gene Marshall, who appeared on the cover as a favor to the composer, a close personal friend who is rumored to be working on a series of new songs for Miss Marshall's next film."

"Midnight Romance" is a symphony of color, sprinkled with rhinestone "stars." The bodice is of satin and tulle in a deep, open V-shape, gathered with self bows at the waist and extending into a long four-point peplum over a skirt of layered tulle in two shades of blue. A wide satin bow adds elegance to the back of the dress. With blue-and-crystal jewelry, hose and matching shoes. "Midnight Romance" is circa 1954, and was designed exclusively for *Gene* by Timothy Alberts.

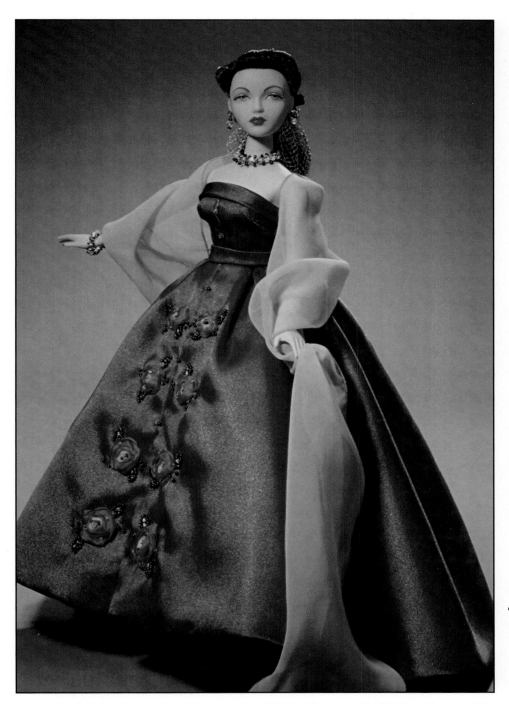

"A Night at Versailles"
1997 FAO Schwarz
Exclusive Doll
Designed by
Timothy Alberts
Original Price $90.00
From card:

"On her recent tour of Europe, actress Gene Marshall attended a gala ball held on the site of the war-ravaged palace at Versailles. Miss Marshall was the most elegant American presence at an event held to benefit the restoration of this magnificient French architectural treasure. Appropriately, she was gowned in the rich purple hues of royalty. It's said that French President Charles DeGaulle was utterly charmed by Miss Marshall's total command of France's language and culture."

Gene is indeed an "elegant presence" in this deep violet satin evening gown accented in lavender, with inverted-pleat tailoring and exquisite beaded ribbon roses detailing the front of the gown. Deep violet evening gloves, lilac chiffon stole, jewlery, shoes, and hose complete the ensemble. Circa 1952. Designed by artist Timothy Alberts for the *Gene Marshall Collection.*

"Warmest Wishes" an F.A.O. Schwarz exclusive. *Gene* carries a gift – a small nutcracker soldier.

$\mathcal{T}$he 1998 $\mathcal{L}$ine

"Crème de Cassis"
>   **1998**
>   **Designed by Timothy Alberts**
>   **Item #94685 (includes doll)**
>   **Original price $79.95**
>   **From card:**

"I'll never forget my interview with Gene Marshall. It was August of '53, and we were sipping crème de cassis cocktails at the Ritz Hotel in Paris. She was wonderful. Witty, intelligent, modest, and utterly lovely. A breath of fresh air. And, ahh, those glorious blue eyes! Luminous, shimmering eyes, enticing me with feminine mystique behind a wispy veil. I fell in love that day."

"Crème de Cassis" is an elegant cocktail ensemble that epitomizes the tasteful flair of an elegant era. A slim lilac bodice and full skirt is overlaid with black lace. Four layers of black and lilac tulle add fullness to the skirt. The belt folds into a large bow. The neckline is accented with a rhinestone-studded bow at the breast. Accessories include a veiled ribbon hat with crystal and black hairpins; "amethyst" and rhinestone jewelry; hose, and velvet strap shoes with rhinestone accents. Circa 1953. Designed by artist Timothy Alberts for the *Gene Marshall Collection.*

"Destiny"
>   **1st Annual Edition Doll –**
>   **Limited to the year 1998**
>   **Designed by Mark Esposito, student designer**
>   **Item #94656 (includes doll)**
>   **Original price $89.95**
>   **From card:**

"Last night fans of Gene Marshall flocked to attend a reception honoring her achievements both on-screen and for children's charities. What a thrill to see the premiere of a newly discovered 'lost reel' of Gene in a never produced 1954 film, 'Destiny.' The clip showed her to flirty perfection in a magnificent ballgown. Gene fans, be sure to catch next month's issue of this magazine for incredible stills from this never-before-seen film!"

"Destiny" is a sumptuous strapless ballgown of dusky teal green taffeta, bordered in gold lamé lace. The attached gold mesh underskirt is double-layered at the hem, allowing the fitted bodice to flow into the full skirt. With evening gloves, barrette, necklace, earrings, and matching shoes. "Destiny" is circa 1954, and was designed exclusively for *Gene* by Mark Esposito, a winner of the 1997 Young Designers of America Student Competition.

Linda Masterson: "We wanted to do an annual edition so that collectors would have something very special from each year. Its not limited in number so that collectors who order early shouldn't have any problem adding the doll for each year to their collection. Of course if they wait too long, it me be sold out!"

"Hello Hollywood Hello"
>   1998
>   **Designed by Doug James**
>   **and Joan Greene**
>   **Item #94657 (includes doll)**
>   **Original price $79.95**
>   **From card:**

"It is this reporter's opinion that famous Hollywood producer Eric von Sternberg has done the world a great favor by discovering Miss Gene Marshall. Reporters greeted her as she stepped off the train today, and it was hard to say who was more dazzled...this small-town beauty with stars in her eyes, or the crowd of hard-nosed reporters who melted under the warmth and sheer star quality of her smile. Miss Marshall's a winner!"

"Hello Hollywood, Hello" is a California-blue, light wool suit trimmed in matching "fur" with a classic, beautifully tailored silhouette. The pencil-thin, kick-pleated skirt is provocatively paired with a fitted "fur"-trimmed jacket over a sleeveless silk blouse with a spill of exquisite lace at the neckline. Accessories include a silk rose bouquet, heart-shaped hat, a blue "fur" muff with hidden lined pocket, gold and rhinestone jewelry, hose, gloves and shoes. Includes a "billboard" by Mel Odom perfect for display. Circa 1941. Designed by Doug James for the *Gene Marshall Collection*.

Dolls of
Excellence
Nominee

"Daughter of the Nile"
>   1998
>   **Designed by Timothy Alberts**
>   **Item #94667 (includes doll)**
>   **Original price $79.95**
>   **From card:**

"Of all the big-name stars glittering in this monumental historic epic, Gene Marshall stands out. Her beautiful portrayal of a visionary priestess of Isis trapped between the Pharoah's will and her destiny of love is exquisitely performed. She expresses a vulnerability over a core of steel that is enthralling. If Cleopatra was anything like Gene, no wonder Rome and Egypt fell at her feet!"

"Daughter of the Nile" is an unforgettable Egyptian gown, reminiscent of the exotic costumes created for the "sweeping historical epic" movies so popular in the 1950's. The fabulous gown is lavishly *handbeaded* with faux gold, turquoise, coral and lapis lazuli on a sheath dress of white silk crepe, lined in a pale silk. Finely pleated, the diaphanous turquoise chiffon robe ripples as fluidly as the Nile. Accessories include gold metallic sandals, handbeaded bracelets, head and armbands and earrings. Circa 1952. Designed by artist Timothy Alberts for the *Gene Marshall Collection*.

"Incognito"
      1998
      Designed by Timothy Alberts
      Item #94659 (includes doll)
      Original price $79.95
      From card:

"Rare glimpses have been reported of Miss Gene Marshall, the famous American cinema star, traveling incognito about Rome and the countryside. I should say, attempting to travel incognito, for what true Italian man could resist the sight of such an extraordinarily beautiful woman in an equally beautiful white Ferrari 375 MM convertible roadster, eh?"

"Incognito" is a carefree summery frock perfect for idling away a sunny afternoon in romantic Italy. The sleeveless halter-style cotton dress is printed in a pretty red floral pattern, with red buttons and organza collar. The fitted bodice hugs *Gene's* curves from bustline to hipline, flaring into a billowing skirt over a crisp cotton petticoat. Accessories include a matching clasp purse with gold chain, a polka-dotted chiffon scarf, sunglasses, nylons, earrings and backless shoes. Circa 1955. Designed by artist Timothy Alberts for the *Gene Marshall Collection*.

"Champagne Supper"
        1998
        Designed by Tim Kennedy
        Item #94662 (includes doll)
        Original price $79.95
        From card:
"Rumors have been flying for years about the wonderful Gene Marshall and a certain very romantic man who has starred with her in a number of films...I think you know of whom I speak, dear readers. But, judging by the expressions on their faces during a candlelit supper at a posh London restaurant, these two are the last to know what I've known all this time...that there's electricity in the air when they're together. Lovebirds at last, hmmm?"

"Champagne Supper" is a sumptuous evening gown of rich copper satin with mahogany "fox" collar and cuffs on the jacket. The bodice fits snugly, flaring with feminine allure over the hips. A corsage of cream roses accents the bodice, while two underlayers of gold netting add fullness to the skirt. Includes golden and amber jewelry, lined clutch purse with chain strap, gloves, nylons and shoes. Circa 1957. Designed by Tim Kennedy for the *Gene Marshall Collection.*

"Forget-Me-Not"
        1998
        Designed by Timothy Alberts
        Item #94653 (costume only)
        Original price $39.95
        From card:
"As the studio's wardrobe mistress, I can tell you for a fact that Gene Marshall's the hardest-working woman in show biz. They had her on a grueling photo shoot schedule that required dozens of costume changes, but she handled it all with a smile...even when everything started going wrong. Other stars would've had fits, but not her. In my opinion, she's one unforgettable lady."

"Forget-Me-Not" is a classic lingerie ensemble from the 1950's that includes a longline bra, panties, fully working garter belt, lace-edged seamed stockings, fluffy mules, a "pearl" necklace and earrings, a satin full slip, and triple-layered tulle crinoline. The accents are superb: satin trim, eyelet lace, tiny satin bows, elastic waistband, and even corset hooks. Dress form, fan and "Dottie" sold separately. Circa 1954. Designed by Timothy Alberts for the *Gene Marshall Collection.*

The entire costume is not pictured.

"Embassy Luncheon"
    1998
    Designed by Laura Meisner
    Item # 94652 (costume only)
    Original price $34.95

"The movie 'Tango' is a must-see! Gene Marshall treats us to a performance that is sure to win a nomination at this year's Golden Star Awards. She positively electrifies the movie theatre during the stunning ballroom scene, standing up to her diplomat father with a passionate intensity that leaves the audiences cheering!"

"Embassy Luncheon" is a compelling, sleek black sheath of wool crepe. Its dramatic appeal lies in the deceptively simple lines that hug every contour. The high standing collar is lavishly hand-embellished with black beads. The matching belt is removable. A back slit allows free movement. The entire dress is fully lined. Accessories include a plush silver fox "fur" stole lined in deep red, petal hat and gloves with black beadwork, drop earrings, nylons, "suede" sling-back heels, and a beaded clutch purse with working snap. Circa 1951. Designed by Laura Meisner for the *Gene Marshall Collection.*

Laura Meisner: "Embassy Luncheon was first seen as a one-of-a-kind at a *Gene* convention."

"Cameo"
    1998
    Designed by Kate Johnson, Student Designer
    Item #94655 (costume only)
    Original price $29.95
    From card:

"Oh look, Esther, it's Katie Marshall with her mother. How nice she's come to our Ladies Fine Arts Society meeting. I used to teach her in the third grade, you know. Quite the performer even then! Who'd have guessed she'd become Gene Marshall, big-time movie star...my, my. But to me she'll always be little Katie who won the school talent competition. Hello Katie dear! My, isn't that a lovely cameo you're wearing."

"Cameo" is a classic '50's gold and white brocade strapless cocktail dress with a sweetheart fitted bodice and short-waisted, cuffed jacket. Both the jacket and dress are fully lined in a peach colored silk. Accessories include a cameo pin attached to the right lapel; gold stud earrings; seamed nude nylons; and matching open-toed shoes. Circa 1951. Designed by Kate Jackson, a winner of the 1997 Young Designers of America Student Competition.

"Gold Sensation"
     1998
     Designed by Tim Kennedy
     Item #94686 (costume only)
     Original price $39.95
     From card:

"Hold the presses, Harry! I've got the hottest fashion news of the Golden Star Awards. Take this down. Gene Marshall, tonight's Best Actress winner, was a showstopper in her gold satin "bubble" gown. But she created a sensation later at the Green Parrot Restaurant when she took off her illusion skirt to reveal a flowing mermaid dress underneath. She's a knockout – literally! Her captivating curves caused a collision between two waiters!"

"Gold Sensation" is a distinctive "bubble gown" ensemble that epitomizes the fashion daring of a fun and frivolous decade. The strapless gold satin gown hugs the figure to the knee, where it bells out in a mermaid train. The matching bubble overskirt is lined in ice blue satin, fastened at the waist with a rhinestone circlet, and again at the knee with a bow. Accessories include a shawl, evening gloves, headpiece, clutch purse, hose, matching shoes with rhinestone buckles, rhinestone circlet earrings. Circa 1957. Designed by Tim Kennedy for the *Gene Marshall Collection.*

Tim Kennedy: "'Gold Sensation' was a tribute to Charles James, the great American designer who was prolific from the 1930s through the 1950s. Balinciaga said that Charles James was the greatest dressmaker in the world because he was an architect in his methods of constuction. During the 1950s and 60s many of the ball gowns worn by women in the Modeste ads were by Charles James. 'Gold Sensation' is a tribute because the shape is architectural, radical and with a sophisticated color combination. The silhouette is exaggerated and its changeable 'convertible' can be worn in more than one way. The whole silhouette changes when you remove the bubble. This was my original design."

"Smart Set"
   1998
   Designed by Doug James
   Item #94687 (costume only)
   Original price $39.95
   From card:

"The scene sent chills down my spine. Gene Marshall is being stalked by a sinister, shadowy figure as she hurries fearfully down the dark colonnaded piazzas of Rome, her missing father's mysterious painting in her arms. The camera captures every subtle nuance of breathless fear and determination that flashes across Gene's expressive face during this unnerving cat-and-mouse game, played out to perfection in this hit movie, 'Montage'."

"Smart Set" is a vibrant, figure-hugging suit dress ensemble. It features a lined, sleeveless sheath dress of red wool crepe, accented with a patterned silk bow. The bolero jacket is lined in matching silk, with a single pleat back for sophisticated drama. Accessories include a black felt chapeau with a white felt feather, gloves, earrings, hose and shoes. Of special note is the original painting by Mel Odom re-created as a miniature print for this costume. Circa 1948. Designed by Doug James for the *Gene Marshall Collection*.

"Love After Hours"
   1998
   Designed by Tim Kennedy
   Item #94658 (costume only)
   Original price $34.95
   From card:

"Have you seen that hilarious new Gene Marshall comedy, 'Personal Secretary'? You've <u>got</u> to see it. There's one scene I love, where her boss tells her she's his date for a VIP client dinner, and gives her only ten minutes to get ready. With help from her friends and some frantic, but ingenious accessorizing, she positively transforms! Wish I could look that great after hours!"

"Love After Hours" is a classic '50s dress of stiff black taffeta. Its deceptively simple lines conceal the superb tailoring details that make this outfit exceptional. The fitted, short-sleeved bodice is lined in shimmering pink organza. Four pleated inset panels let the full skirt swirl with feminine grace. An extra 3" shirred layer adds fullness to the pink organza crinoline. Accessories include a golden-edged fan, silk flowers, "pearl" necklace and earrings, evening gloves, hose and matching shoes. Circa 1957. Designed by artist Tim Kennedy for the *Gene Marshall Collection*.

"Midnight Angel"
> **1998**
> **Designed by Nicole Burke, Student designer**
> **Item #94674 (costume only)**
> **Original price $39.95**
> **From card:**

"'Love's Ghost' was released today to record crowds. Miss Gene Marshall stars in this gothic love story about a governess haunted by a romantic ghost in a dark Victorian mansion on the Yorkshire moors. You'll be thrilled and chilled when she races onto the dangerous moors at night to find a lost boy, lured to safety by the eerie beckoning of her ghost."

"Midnight Angel" is a treasure of meticulous detail. The pale rose cotton dress features leg-o-mutton sleeves, lace collar, detachable cummerbund, a "looping" applique, and full netted crinoline. The navy blue wool coat is edged with gold piping along the hem and Edwardian-style cape. Gold and black bows accent the back. The coat and dress are fully lined. The tie bonnet is trimmed in gold brocade, black chenille and gold cord. With shoes, hose, "pearl" earrings and rose brooch. Circa 1946. Designed by Nicole Burke, a winner of the 1997 Young Designers of American Student Competition.

"Hi-Fi"
> **1998**
> **Designed by Doug James**
> **Item #94669 (costume only)**
> **Original price $34.95**
> **From card:**

"In our candid interview with Miss Gene Marshall, she was the perfect hostess, taking us on an informal tour of her enchanting Beverly Hills villa. It was an intriguing glimpse into this star's personal life: her interests and hobbies outside of films. Her vast record collection is almost as extensive as her musical acumen."

"Hi-Fi" is a casual ensemble perfect for relaxing around the house. The avocado green sleeveless silk blouse is lined with white organza, and accented with handsewn "amber" beads. The matching sweater has ¾ inch sleeves, decorative buttons, and finished ribbing at the waist. The Capri pants are brown wool worsted gabardine, fitted with darts. Includes "topaz" drop earrings, hair bandeau, "gold" bracelet, and shoes. Of special note is the miniature "Blue Evening" album jacket and record. Circa 1954. Designed by artist Doug James for the *Gene Marshall Collection.*

"Safari"
 1998
 Designed by Timothy Alberts
 Item #94673 (costume only)
 Original price $39.95
 From card:
"OK, Miss Marshall, this African sun is really hot, so we'll wrap this photo shoot up with one for the front cover. Put those sunglasses on so you don't squint. Nix the pith helmet this time and lemme see you in the scarf. OK now, let's have a big wave for the fans back home. Good, terrific shot! It's a wrap. Let's get into the shade pronto. Miss Marshall, it's a pleasure to work with a real pro like you!"

"Safari" is Hollywood's idea of a "practical" safari ensemble! The khaki bush jacket is of a cotton linen blend, with buttons and a "leopard" pattern lining the jacket and front pockets. A unique pleat and belt accent adds flair to the back. The sleeveless white cotton fitted blouse features a high collar and buttons. The khaki cotton linen slacks close at the back. Accessories include a pith helmet, removable belt, jet earrings, sunglasses, shoes, and a leopard patterned chiffon scarf. Circa 1951. Designed by artist Timothy Alberts for the *Gene Marshall Collection.*

"Rain Song"
 1998
 Designed by Doug James
 Item #94675 (costume only)
 Original price $29.95
 From card:
"Though I was only eight years old when I starred in the film 'Rain Song' with Gene Marshall, I still can remember every smile, every hug, every laugh I shared with her. Just like my character in the movie, I too had a secret crush on her. What a beautiful, loving woman. She made me feel like I was the smartest, handsomest, most wonderful boy on earth. I still have a crush on her!"

"Rain Song" is a lovely pale rose hooded raincoat of a slubbed silk and linen blend. Fully lined in a patterned pink and gray lining, it fastens down the front with pink buttons. The belt is removable, and the hood attaches beneath the collar with buttons. Accessories include quarter-length gray gloves with tiny button details, a gray and white patterned scarf, "pearl" earrings, a miniature newspaper, black shoes, and gray nylon "galoshes" that fasten over the shoes with white bead buttons. Circa 1953. Designed by artist Doug James for the *Gene Marshall Collection.*

"On the Avenue"
FAO Schwarz Spring Exclusive Doll, LE 5,000
1998
Designed by Tim Kennedy
Item #94668
Issue price $90.00
From card:

"It's a toss-up as to what's making New York City look so beautiful today, the perfect sunshine or the radiant Miss Gene Marshall, in town for a big publicity event at the Plaza. Gene surprised reporters by showing up on foot accompanied only by a large stuffed bunny she says she bought for a six year old fan. She told this reporter that the day was so beautiful she just had to leave the limo behind and take a walk along the Avenue. Sounds like a great idea to me."

"On the Avenue" is the perfect afternoon ensemble to enjoy a warm New York City day. The soft green color is reminiscent of a minty ice cream parfait, sewn of breezy silk chiffon. A picture hat sprigged with flowers and a "pearl" hatpin shades her face. Gloves, matching strap sandals, a necklace, bracelet and earrings of "peridot" stones and "gold" complete this lovely ensemble. Circa 1955. Designed by artist Tim Kennedy for the *Gene Marshall Collection.*

Tim Kennedy: "Mel and I called this outfit 'Parfait' because it is such an ice cream color. It was taken from a *Vogue* magazine from the 1940s or 50s. In the magazine it was a lavender color – the gloves, shoes, and dress were all the same color. It was all one dreamy pastel color. The hat in the original had no flowers" Since there was already lavender in the *Gene* line, in "Crème de Cassis" and "Prominade," it was decided to do this outfit in a different color. "There is a lot of resistance to green in market testing, but this is a non-threatening shade of green." Another reason for changing the color of an outfit is the "commercial aspect, the harmonious balance (of the line). A garment color will change if it is discordant with the others since they are displayed together. As a designer I do what I love, and sometimes things get changed." "'On the Avenue' was originally designed to be part of the line, not designed as an exclusive."

Gene in "Warmest Wishes"
An FAO Schwarz Fall Exclusive Doll
Designed by Tim Kennedy
Item #94663 (doll and costume)
Original price $110.00
From card:

See Opposite Page

"Dear Miss Marshall:
Thank you for the toy soldier you gave me for Christmas. He's proudly standing an honor guard on my table where I can see him all the time. Your kindness in taking time to pick out a thoughtful gift for an old, war-shot doorman, gives me the warmest feeling in my heart when I stand outside in my uniform on cold winter days...just like this soldier. With deepest regards; Henry Cooper"

"Warmest Wishes" is a rust-colored knit dress with a pocket below the belt. A teal green chiffon cowl and hip sash accents the dress, with a gold brooch for the scarf. Her toasty-warm winter coat is lined in taffeta, flaring below the knee. A twist-style hat curves over one ear. With matching muff, closed-toe "suede" shoes, gift box with toy soldier, hose and "aquamarine" earrings. Her reddish-umber hair is in a classic 1940s style. Circa 1948. Designed by artist Tim Kennedy for the *Gene Marshall Collection."*

"Midnight Gamble"
   Gene Authorized Retailer's Exclusive,
      LE 9,500
   1998
   Designed by Doug James
   Item #94666 (doll included)
   Original price $99.95
   From card:

"Lady Luck must be a big fan of the so-beautiful American cinema star, Gene Marshall. After enjoying a private viewing of painter Jacques Zoli's new exhibit, Miss Marshall and her date were seen at Le Rouge et Le Noir casino club around midnight. The roulette wheel must be a fan, too, for Gene, who had never gambled before, won big against the house, much to everyone's delight."

"Midnight Gamble"is a sleek sheath of navy blue crepe lined in white knit. Three pleats of a Prussian blue silk highlight the bodice, draping from a knot into shashes accented with silver metallic embroidery, sequins and beads. The trapeze-style jacket is of matching blue silk, with white patterned silk lining, inverted back pleat, and three-quarter sleeves with cuffs. Lavishly hand-embellished with sequins, beads and silver metallic embroidery, it includes gloves, silver shoes and earrings. Circa 1953. Designed by artist Doug James for the *Gene Marshall Collection.*

"Ransom in Red"
        Retailer's Exclusive, LE 7,500
                for Christmas 1998
        Designed by Tim Kennedy
        Item #94676 (costume only)
        Original price $44.95
        From card:

"The 'Ransom in Red' perfume campaign featuring the dazzling Miss Gene Marshall, has hit the air waves and magazine shelves just in time for the peak holiday buying season. Judging by the long lines at perfume counters, men are willing captives to Miss Marshall's breathless whisper, red lips and sultry blue eyes!"

"Ransom in Red" is a firey red peplum sheath dress with an unconventional design. The halter bodice extends into an unusual split train that unfurls like poinsettia petals a full 13" down from the waist. The svelte skirt has a single slit up the back to the knee. *Gene* is wearing a king's ransom of jewels, including a "ruby and pearl" bracelet and three-tiered "diamond" earrings. Includes gloves, hose and red grosgrain ribbon strap shoes. Circa 1949. Designed by artist Tim Kennedy for the *Gene Marshall Collection.*

Tim Kennedy: "'Ransom in Red' was based on a 1940s dress pictured in a magazine. It may have been an illustration by the French artist Rene Gruau who did the Chanel ads. The drawing was of a column evening gown with a peplum. I thought it needed something distinctive, so I made the peplum continue in back in panels that became a train that made it look very sculptural, very graceful."

Gene in "Covent Garden"
The Parkwest/NALED Exclusive Doll
Designed by Tim Kennedy
Item #94664
Issue price $99.95
From card:

"Cinderella arrives at the ball! The famous American cinema star, Miss Gene Marshall, continues her royal visit to London with an evening at Covent Garden Opera House to see Rossini's 'La Cenerentola', the story of Cinderella, Miss Marshall epitomizes the classic fairytale, not only with her own rags-to-riches story, but in a fabulous evening gown that would make even England's 2-week old baby prince fall madly in love at first sight!"

"Covent Garden" is an extravagant floor-length evening gown that floats in a dreamlike cloud of opalescent white satin and snow white tulle. A lace-up bodice of black velvet leads into a bow and sash train. An opera cape of rich black velvet lined in white satin, a velvet choker with silk blossoms, and "pearls" completes this splendid vision of a storybook heroine arriving at the ball. Circa 1948. Designed by artist Tim Kennedy for the *Gene Marshall Collection*.

Tim Kennedy: "'Covent Garden' is very Aubrey Beardsley, very black and white. It was my response to an assignment to do something in black and white. It is very much inspired by the 1860's period, with a corselet kind of waist and the shape of the skirt. But it is also very 1940's with the clothing influence of the 19th century, like 'Gone With the Wind." I like the snood. The outfit is ethereal and romantic. It is all my original design. I love that it is so emphatic black and white with one accent color. I used a pink rose in 'Covent Garden' because it needed an ethereal color, not a harsh color."

119

The Present & Future Dream

"Simply *Gene*" 1999 Doll
Item #93526, redhead; #93527, blonde;
#93528, brunette
Original price $49.95

Joan Greene: "*Gene* has become more bendable, more playable, more poseable, and a little less like a fine statue. But 'Simply *Gene*' has been wildly successful, people absolutely love her."

The decision was made to not style "Simply *Gene's*" hair, but to give her long hair so that collectors would have what they asked for.

Ann Parsons, a collector and former doll dealer with whom Mel discussed his concept before *Gene* was made into a doll, says "I am glad to see that *Gene* finally has articulated legs and hair that can be styled. Those were first on my list when we were talking about her design."

The sun suit, designed by Joan Greene, is based on a real bathing suit from Valentino's. "It was the quintessential sort of late 40s and early 50s bathing suit. I was risqué at the time to show a bit of midriff. Shon Le Blanc, owner of Valentino's, was kind enough to send us the real suit to us."

The most exciting news for 1999 was that *Gene* has bendable legs. "The shining star in 99 was the introduction of 'Simply *Gene*,'" Linda Masterson states. The three "Simply *Gene*" dolls give collectors less expensive dolls to dress in *Gene's* wonderful costumes and her bendable knees make life-like posing and sitting easier. Her longer "unstyled" hair encourages collectors to have fun changing her hairstyle, too.

"We do constantly listen to what collectors say they want, and we try really hard to deliver it," Joan Greene stresses. "We heard loud and clear that they wanted *Gene* to have knees that bent. The thing that Mel and I agreed with wholeheartedly was that, although *Gene* is a modern doll, she has that nostalgic feeling. She certainly speaks of the 1940s and 50s, so we wanted her knees to be in keeping with the way joints would have been made on dolls during that time." Ashton-Drake counted on the Director of their office in Asia, David Murray, to help accomplish this.

Mel Odom says that the 1999 line is "one of our strongest, ever. The diversity amazed me – from Army uniforms to evening gowns."

An interesting development for 1999 was the strong historical theme in the line of dolls and costumes. Collectors were delighted that one doll, several costumes and an accessory pack were designed with stories relating to *Gene's* USO tour of England and France during World War II. Masterson says that "World War II was the last good war – the country was united, everyone made sacrifices willingly, everyone was behind it." Putting *Gene* in that setting dimensionalizes her as a person – she put herself in peril like many Hollywood stars did.

A major reality for *Gene* is that a time is

being depicted that actually existed. "We are trying to be as faithful to the 1940s and 50s as we can be," Joan Greene explains. "These pieces in many ways did exist, so it is almost what a modern designer's   interpretation can be, how they can add their little stamp to a Dior-like suit or a Balenciaga-type evening gown, but make it theirs. That is part of the charm and part of the difficulty." Obviously a great deal of research went into many of the costumes and accessories. Doug James, designer of "USO," says "*Gene* is a period doll and the designs for her outfits must come from somewhere. They have to be appropriate for those times. You can't just make them up."

"The other side of the coin is that *Gene* is a movie star," Joan Greene adds. "During the war when fabric was rationed, Edith Head used the fabric she had hoarded, like people who love fabric do, for the movies. Movies were made for everyone's entertainment. Although you might remake your father's suit into a dress or a suit to wear, you could go to the movies and see the most wonderful lush evening gowns and big skirts. That is one of the beauties of *Gene* – we can dream dreams and she can wear them, because she is a movie star."

In addition to the nearly three dozen new dolls and costumes, Ashton-Drake Galleries introduced a whole range of new products, including *Gene* furniture, jewelry, original music and videos. The video contains two songs: "She'd Rather Dance" written and performed by Mel Odom, and "Share the Dream"(*Gene's* Theme) written by David R. Lehman, Joan Greene and Linda Masterson. Both songs are on the CD as well, along with classic songs that were on the billboard top 100 in the 1940s and 50s.

The furniture, in particular, helps collectors make *Gene's* world come to life. *Gene's* new bedroom furniture includes a classic sleigh bed and a 1940's-style dresser, both with a swan motif. The inspiration for the top of the dresser was an artists' easel the shape of the mirror. According to Joan Greene, the idea was that the furniture could have been on the set of a movie that *Gene* particularly loved or that *Gene* mentioned she would like furniture with this sort of motif to a furniture maker who built the pieces for her. The pillows are monogrammed, too, sophisticated and low key, in thread to match the fabric.

The new accessories range from a panther lamp and director's chair to jewelry. Greene says that one of the things Ashton-Drake tries to do with the collection is to help people mix and match from one season to the next. "In the 1950s they turned everything into lamps. The panther was a popular what-not of the day, so we turned it into a lamp. The "Safari" costume is lined with a little leopard print similar to the lampshade -- so the lamp could accessorize a safari set."

"*Gene* is not a doll to people, she is a doorway to creativity and self-expression, to a more glamorous, fanciful life than any of us get to lead today," explains Masterson. "That's why we started her furniture – it makes it more of a world. She's not a doll, she has a life. These items expand the fantasy." The music CD and video also are a doorway since, "Music sets the mood so beautifully and was so much a part of life then."

A side note to *Gene's* popularity: the two Vogue patterns introduced this summer, for a suit (V311) and an evening gown (V312), are Vogue's number one selling patterns.

There were personnel changes for 1999 in the *Gene* Team, with both new members and new titles. Linda Masterson, Director, emphasizes that the expanded team is still small in relation to other companies. "Mattel probably has more people working on *Barbie's*® eyelashes than we have on our whole team!"

Mel Odom with Joan Greene and Linda Masterson.

Top row: Kirk Swenk, three "Simply Genes," Frank Rotundo. Bottom row: Wendy Solomon, Linda Masterson, Julie Najawicz, and Dee Golfinopoulos.

Yerman Romaro and Patti Hojnacki.

David Murray and Lisa Maurino.

New titles this year included Joan Greene's promotion to Director, Frank Rotundo to Product Development Manager, and Wendy Solomon to Team Coordinator. Beth Maxwell continues as Retail Marketing Manager. New members of the *Gene* Team are Dee Golfinopoulos, Art Director; Kirk Swenk, Senior Writer; Julie Najawicz, Associate Product Development Manager; and Luredia Kinnard, Client Services Representative. Dee creates the catalogs, mailings, postcards, signs, even the buttons that *Gene* fans covet. Kirk is a film, theatre and trivia buff, the perfect person to be *Gene's* wordsmith. Julie helps develop *Gene's* stunning wardrobe and many of the accessories. Luredia is the person who listens to the opinions of *Gene* collectors.

Lisa Maurino and Ed Bailey-Mershon are responsible for the actual production of *Gene* dolls, costumes and accessories. David Murray is the overseas Production Director who oversees the day-to-day process of producing the *Gene* products. Others who have been important as design team members are Patty Hojnacki, *Gene's* hairstylist; George Sarafen, a new designer for 2000; Yerman Romaro, costume duplication; Kim Fisher, jewelry designer; and Dennis Gibbons, prop design.

"Overall the 99 collection reflects what collectors have told us about what they want. It is a balance between fantasy roles and period clothes, between tailored and elegant, between slinky (dresses) and ball gowns... all the things people said they wanted as long as they are in keeping with the *Gene* story," explains Masterson.

What can we look forward to for *Gene's* fifth birthday? It is bound to be exciting! Mel is working on a biography of *Gene* to be published by Hyperion Press. He is writing the story of *Gene* as well as drawing many of the illustrations for the book. Also, fans have been asking for another female character or a male character long enough that one may be a possibility. There's no question that *Gene's* universe is expanding. Hints are that the dolls, costumes and accessories for the coming year are outstanding. As Linda Masterson promises, "2000 is the beginning of a new millenium and a bright future for *Gene*."

"Song of Spain"
      1999 Annual Edition Doll
      Designed by Tim Kennedy
      Item #76065
      Original price $99.95
      Story:

In the 1943 movie Sea Spree, Gene Marshall performed a white-hot flamenco dance number "Song of Spain." "It was so difficult and daring that the 24 beautiful toreador dancers were complaining. But everyone gasped when the demanding choreographer told Gene to unfasten her mock skirt and reattach it around her neck as a matador's cape…while in full spin down a narrow, steep flight of slippery marble steps! "Impossible! Don't do it, Gene!" cried the dancers, but Gene was silent. With a frown of concentration, she mounted the stairs and slowly worked out the necessary moves.

When the cameras rolled, Gene spun down the stairs. Her radiant smile never faltered. Halfway, the skirt billowed off in a dazzling flourish of gold, black and scarlet, only to be swept close again as she fastened it to her neck on the next three perilous turns.

"Song of Spain" is a magnificent fantasy of a matador costume in black and gold brocade, fully lined with gold satin, circa 1943. The daring halter top features ornate golden beads that dangle enticingly over *Gene's* bare midriff. Golden Beads accent both the figure-hugging toreador pants and bolero jacket. The dashing circle cape is of gold brocade lined with scarlet satin. It doubles as a full-length skirt. The outfit includes a matador's hat with a long stemmed red rose, shoes and golden hoop earrings. *Gene's* spice-dark hair is neatly rolled up into a snood of gold net.

Tim Kennedy: " 'Song of Spain' is my favorite accomplishment for *Gene* – it is so completely unique, the kind of thing that would have been done for a musical number. Also, it has play quality – there are so many looks with four simple pieces and they all look good. This was originally designed to be the 98 convention doll. When Ashton-Drake saw it, they realized it needed to be more widely available. So it was traded with another already in the 99 line since the time was too short to have one delivered in time for the convention. At the signing at FAO, one collector commented 'Finally! A costume!' The whole outfit popped into my head one night: the long brocade gown and *Gene* spinning down the steps when she flips it inside out and it becomes a matador's cape."

Mel Odom: " 'Song of Spain' is one of my favorite things we've done. When Timmy came to me at first with the idea, I didn't get it at first – a matador? The he said, 'the skirt comes off and becomes a cape, and the cape can be reversed and you can have a red skirt or a brocade skirt. And the jacket comes off and you have a little bolero under it and the skirt and bolero looks like an evening gown, or you can have it with just the toreador pants and top – it's like seven or eight different outfits."

"USO"

1999 Doll
Designed by Doug James
Item #76061
Original price $79.95
Story:

From July through early August of 1944 Gene performed the demanding role of a USO/ Camp Shows volunteer, touring the perilous Foxhole Circuit to boost the morale of American fighting men on the front lines. She was one of the "Soldiers in Greasepaint," bringing laughter and a bit of home to war-weary men and women while bombs exploded just a few miles away. The GIs loved her.

To maintain military secrecy, Gene was not allowed to reveal her itinerary to anyone. Her troupe traveled in England and France, performing 14 shows a week in castles, the back of supply trucks, and on hastily thrown-together stages in the middle of cow fields and combat zones. The soldiers' courage and patriotism made Gene so proud to wear the uniform that the studio had made for her – not too authentic, so the enemy would realize she wasn't a soldier if she were captured. These two months were the hardest...and proudest...days of her life.

"USO" is the studio's version of a dress uniform representative of all the branches of the military, circa 1944. The tailored jacket is of a dark green wool and features brass buttons down the front and on the breast pockets and epaulets. The jacket, belt and skirt are lined in green taffeta. The khaki cotton long-sleeved shirt features a matching necktie. Accessories include earrings, a "leather" strap purse lined in taffeta, a wool garrison cap, hose, and "leather" lace-up boots. *Gene's* chestnut hair is styles in a bouncy flip.

Doug James: "World War II was the major event in *Gene's* life. To have something that directly ties her to the war is important. It was difficult to research 'USO,' especially to find the exact shade of green the uniforms were. Most photos are black and white, and you can't trust the color in the old color photos. Even looking at the real WAC uniforms (is deceiving) because the fabric had faded over time. In 'USO' I made it more of a golden khaki color, not quite army green. I added a box pleat to the front, which was used on certain uniforms. I wanted it to be real. I spent a lot of time researching real WAC uniforms and it is as authentic as I could make it." The designer says there were some changes from the prototype: "I had intended for the microphone to come with the doll. I found a small photo of FDR and shrunk it down to fit in *Gene's* purse (which is the exact official style), and even researched his handwriting and put at the bottom of his picture 'To Miss Marshall, with thanks, FDR.' I had wanted it to come with a set of three miniature war bond posters – they would be wonderful as a display venue."

Mel Odom: "I'm thrilled that 'USO' is in the line. The whole series of costumes we did around the USO trip are very story driven. I think it is nice to acknowledge that movie stars really did do something wonderful during the war effort. It is something we have a difficult time understanding now because our culture is so different, but Hollywood was a patriotism machine during the war. It was a way of keeping the country together."

Joan Greene: "This was made as authentic as we can. It is officially licensed by the USO, and designed by Doug James. World War II did happen during the time that *Gene* represents, and we don't pretend that it didn't. We have put a doll in the line that would have been very much in keeping with what a movie star would have done during the war. She wouldn't have gone to war per se, but she would have supported the effort by selling war bonds. She might very likely have entertained the troops just as Bob Hope and Joan Crawford and many other famous stars did at the time. We've kept *Gene's* history true to the times."

Linda Masterson: "The Special Edition of 'USO' made for the signing at FAO has an authentic armband, which was worn by all USO volunteers, and a pin for her hat."

124

"Love, Paris"
1999 Doll
Designed by Jose Ferrand
Item #76063
Original price $79.95
Story:

When Gene received two large packages from Paris, she was surprised to open the first and find a jacket and circle skirt of the softest, dove gray silk tweed with dashing black accents. Drawing it out, she gasped...what an innovative fashion design! A fine vellum letter fluttered out from the sweeping folds of the skirt. The note read "You are an inspiration, a breath of fresh air. I hope you like wearing my newest fashion. Love, Paris."

The second box contained an elegant rose suede hat and accessories to complement the outfit perfectly. Gene wore this remarkable fashion creation to the orphan's charity fundraiser the next afternoon and the press went wild when she walked into the room. The media attention made it the most successful fundraiser ever. Gene's secret admirer never came forward... but every year after that, Gene unfailingly sent a bouquet of perfect pink roses to a certain famous Paris designer in gratitude and admiration.

"Love Paris" is a stunning example of the innovative New Look that defined post-war fashion, circa 1947. The jacket and flowing circle skirt are of gray silk tweed lined with gray satin. The fitted, long-sleeved jacket features black mock pockets and collar, with a black lace and petal accent. An underskirt of ruffled black organza provides fullness and lift to the skirt. Accessories include a rose "suede" hat and purse, pink rhinestone drop earrings, hose and lace-up shoes. *Gene's* ash-blonde hair is styles in a double French twist.

Jose Ferrand: "'Love, Paris' is one of the costumes that I originally showed Mel It was inspired by a photograph of my mother and seven of her friends that had been taken in 1947, a few months before her graduation—she was 17. She and her friends are wearing the new long dresses shown by Christian Dior in his debut collection only four months before. Very clearly neither my mother or her friends would ever look the same – they seemed to be embracing their womanhood in a new era of elegance. It is a photograph that captured my imagination as a child because this New Look was so absolute that it rendered everything in your closet obsolete. My mother's suit was the one that epitomized the new look the best. I added the black accents and changed the hat to make it more dramatic."

Mel Odom: "I'm very proud of 'Love, Paris.' It's an amazing job of tailoring and it's based on an outfit that Jose's mother wore. She received her 'Love, Paris' on Mother's Day and wrote me the sweetest note about how much it touched her and that people bring their life's experience and use *Gene* to express it. I'm thrilled that a fond memory was used as the basis for an outfit... there's a lot of emotion based on triggering those memories with an object. *Gene* being an object – if you can believe that! We made 'Love, Paris' a doll rather than a costume because it is such a distinct silhouette."

Joan Greene: "'Love, Paris' is one of my favorite outfits this year. It speaks so eloquently of what happened in the world of fashion right after the war. America had been used to having their fashions dictated by Europe, by Paris. When the war came, the American designers got to come to the forefront since the European designers were very cut off. With the New Look of Christian Dior, the French designers came back with a roar. And women in America went from wearing outfits regulated by the war -- they were told the size of their hems, how many pockets they could have, how wide their skirt could be-- to the New Look."

"She'd Rather Dance"
1999 Doll
Designed by Tim Kennedy
Item #76062
Original price $79.95
Story:

In the flamboyantly colorful Technicolor film "She'd Rather Dance" Gene played the high-spirited daughter of an old distinguished Boston family. Gene loved to dance and at every party Gene was always on the ballroom floor. But when a Broadway producer spotted her dancing at a cotillion and asked her to star in his new show, her family was horrified when she said yes.

The showstopper of the Broadway show (and the film) "She'd Rather Dance" was the title song in which a chorus line of tuxedoed men sang in Gene's honor..."But if you want a chance at romance, ask her to dance." Gene emerged into the spotlight in a vibrant frosted tangerine dress with a plumed hat and dramatic long shawl. She proceeded to dance a different dance step, from turkey trot to a tarantella, with every man in the chorus. The audiences went wild and the family was reconciled for the brightest of all technicolor endings!

"She'd Rather Dance" is a sizzling sheath dress in a glorious frosty tangerine color, circa 1948. Created of tangerine orange satin, the strapless "V"-cut bodice sparkles with sequins and beads. The matching sheath skirt has a knee-high slit, the hem curled to reveal the silk lining. A spectacular stole in matching silk and satin adds dramatic excitement. Accessories include a matching hat with dyed feather, gold mesh belt and shoes, golden link earrings, necklaces and gloves. *Gene's* dark hair is bound in a golden ribbon.

Tim Kennedy: " This was based on a 1940's illustration by Jacques Fath, but a great amount of liberty was taken in interpreting it since in the illustration you can't tell what is really going on. I didn't see a photograph of the actual garment. The illustration wasn't colored, so the strong color was based on the success of 'Tango.' "

Mel Odom: "I like 'She'd Rather Dance' without the hat. I like it better with the shawl over the head – it's very East Indian-looking. The dress is a tricky little thing. It looks like it's got a peplum except the peplum actually swerves back into the skirt – it doesn't go all the way around the dress. It is a particularly beautiful couple shades of orange. I picked it to be photographed with just because I thought the color was so wonderful."

Opposite Page:
"Savannah"
1999 Doll
Designed by Katie McHale, a winner of the Ashton-Drake Young Designers of America competition
Item #76064
Original price $79.95
Story:

Gene stars in "Look Away, Look Away," a saga of a simpler South where chivalry was the order of the day. Gene is the heroine who, after her mother's untimely death, assumes her duties, from running the plantation in Savannah for her politician father and serving as his hostess to raising her twin sisters and finding them suitable husbands.

In a flashback, we see Gene before the mantel of responsibility was placed on her shoulders. Coquettish and carefree, lovely in green and fawn, all the handsome young men seek her favor. But the glance of one man, when their eyes met across the Bougainvillea, etched itself into her memory.

But duties call and her father's first guests for today's reception are being announced – including that of a Northern gentleman from Ashtabula whose name she doesn't remember from the guest list...

"Savannah" is an off-the-shoulder gown, circa 1860. The full-length fawn-colored moiré underskirt is accented by a green moiré train that suggests a bustle. The green moiré bodice ends in a short apron overskirt, cut at the waist by a ribbon sash. The overskirt sports decorations of gathered ribbons and ribbon rosettes. The bodice features a white organza gathered trim, embroidered with white braiding intermingled with crocheted pink roses with green "leaves." The ensemble includes "pearl" earrings, green shoes, and cream-colored ribbon rosettes for *Gene's* dark hair, which cascades in ringlets.

Mel Odom: "This is a student design that went into the line exactly as she designed it. It was the most perfect of any of the original student costumes I've ever seen personally – just perfect. The hairdo by Frank Rotundo is different from her design, but everything else is exactly the same."

Below Right:
"Lucky Stripe"
     1999 Doll
     Designed by Tim Kennedy
     Item #93529
     Original price $79.95
     Story:

"Bird of Paradise" has wrapped for a long weekend and Gene has decided, on the spur of the moment, to get away from the glare of studio lights. She puts on her "lucky" outfit and in a quick call to her agent, is told she's been offered the lead in "Monaco." At the train station, the porter takes her valise and advises that "Palm Springs is awfully pretty this time of year..." At the ticket window the clerk says, "Miss Marshall, you're in luck – the train for Palm Springs leaves in ten minutes." Then she adds, "Plus there's a private compartment available!" At the hotel in Palm Springs, the desk clerk says the hotel is booked, "However, as luck would have it, we do have a small guest house on the outskirts of the grounds available…" How lucky can one girl get?

"Lucky Stripe" is a smartly tailored afternoon ensemble, circa 1949. The square-necked dress is horizontally striped in black and taupe with long sleeves and a narrow knee-length skirt. *Gene's* skirt is asymmetrically draped onto one hip with a falling panel of vertical stripes. A large, uniquely-styles black satin hat matches the black satin drum-shaped purse, with a golden bead closure and golden detail on the handle. Short red gloves add a flash of color. The outfit includes "onyx" teardrop earrings; hose; and black sling-back shoes. *Gene's* long blonde hair is swept back and gathered with a braided knot.

Tim Kennedy: "This was inspired by a Lucianna Long dinner dress illustration. It was originally going into the line as a costume, but it was a favorite of the CEO at Ashton-Drake and was put into the line as a doll."

Mel Odom: "Lucky Stripe was a fashion illustration that I showed to Timmy and got him to interpret. After he did it, I thought in cinematic terms and added the red gloves so that everything else would be beige and black – the only color on the hands. (In a movie) of course you would watch their hands whatever they did."

"Stand Up and Cheer"
1999 Costume
Designed by Dolly Cipolla
Item #76070
Original price $44.95
Period ca 1944
Story:

A week after D-Day, Gene and her fellow USO Camp Tour entertainers found themselves on a transport boat cutting across the English Channel to Normandy, the new front lines. During their first show there, Gene could see the hope dawning in the faces of the soldiers she met. The tide of war was turning in the Allies' favor at long last, and a fresh new spirit was budding in everyone's heart. Gene and the famous comedian USO host decided that she would perform her patriotic new number for the finale, hoping it would spark morale to a bright new flame.

Gene stepped out from the wings with the energy of a sizzling firecracker, high-kicking and belting out a rousing song for America, the flag and the 4th of July. Thousands of booted feet started to stop with the beat, thousands of hands clapped with enthusiasm. A fresh, brisk breeze blew from the west, and set the American flag to waving proudly over their heads. An electrifying feeling swept through the audience and by the end, every soldier was on his feet, cheering for the red, white and blue!

"Stand Up and Cheer" is a bold dance costume as colorful, dazzling and patriotic as the 4th of July. The blue satin coat with tails has gleaming gold lamé at the cuffs, lapels, belt and lining. Gold stars accent the back bow and tails. The stretchy leotard is spangled with applied pailettes. Of special note are the fancy fishnet pantyhose with star-shaped red sequins along the calf. Red and white "leather" boots reach mid-shin, and feature blue embroidery, gold trim and bootstraps. Accessories include "ruby" and star drop earrings, a matching top hat, and a "firecracker" hand prop.

Dolly Cipolla: " The original of this was one of 50 showgirls sent to FAO (for the store opening in Las Vegas). It was lost in shipping, but FAO found it and donated it back two years ago for Ashton-Drake to auction off for GMHC. When the original, which was burgandy, was lost, I made a second version in red, white and blue out of suede and leather. The (final mass-produced) version couldn't use the suede and leather, but the fit came back so beautiful – it is exactly like what we sent. The boots look great with the little gold edging. This is one of the dolls that little girls really like!"

Mel Odom: "This has the most incredible little cowboy boots I have ever seen for a doll. The outfit is astonishing because of those boots – they're made of leatherette and slip easily on and off the feet."

Opposite Page Bottom:
"Farewell Golden Moon"
1999 Costume
Designed by Tim Kennedy
Item #76067
Original price $44.95
Period ca 1944
Story:

"Farewell golden moon, for my love is gone away..."

Gene traveled through England and France the summer of 1944 entertaining the troops on the perilous Foxhole Circuit of the USO Camp Shows.

"I wished on every star for him to come home..."

They traveled like gypsies from camp to camp, making do with what rough comforts they had. They performed on makeshift stages in the middle of cow fields or on supply trucks. They sang boogie-woogie tunes, danced, got laughs with hilarious comedy sketches...but nothing touched them like Gene's "Farewell Golden Moon."

"The night is too long without my love beside me..."

Whenever Gene sang the heart-aching ballad of a lonely woman who years for her love to come home, the GIs saw in her their own special girl waiting at home, praying for his safe return. In that twilight realm between civilization and war, Gene shown incandescent with memories, hope and the golden promise of love and devotion.

"So farewell golden moon, 'til his arms are around me again."

"Farewell Golden Moon" is a luminous evening gown shimmering with romance. The halter-style bodice is of gold lamé, and features a wide, star-pointed waistband. The gold lamé of the bodice extends into a full-length skirt which gleams under a misty overskirt of creamy soft tulle. Both the bodice and skirt are fully lined. A long tulle wrap attaches to the bodice with a golden and "Pearl" brooch. Accessories include earrings, ¾ length gloves with "pearls" at the wrist, shoes, hose, and a "pearl" and gold laurel wreath headpiece.

Tim Kennedy: "This was inspired by an actual dress designed by Irene for a department store."

Mel Odom: "I love 'Farewell Golden Moon' as an evening gown. It was one of the first things ever designed for *Gene* back when she was only plaster. It's one of the outfits that I showed when I presented *Gene* as a concept and have wanted to put in the line, and this year it fit."

"Press Conference"
1999 Costume
Designed by
Dolly Cipolla
Item #76068
Original price
$44.95
Period ca 1944
Story:

Gene Marshall's name was at the top of the list of stars from Monolithic Studios who were to be sent on tour with the USO Camp Shows. For Gene, although the publicity would be sensational, it was unimportant next to the opportunity to bring a little bit of home to the boys fighting on the front. At the press conference announcing her upcoming USO tour, Gene stood poised and proud between the USO sign and the American flag. "We are soldiers without guns, she said. "Your contributions, your sacrifices, both large and small, are just as vital to winning the war as the soldiers fighting up on the front lines. Do your part, and together we'll bring our boys home victorious."

"Press Conference" is a two-piece fitted day suit, circa 1944. The short sleeved collarless top is a pale peach waffle pattern wool lined in peach chiffon. It is accented with an open V-neck and a ribbon corsage. Four appliqued stripes of brown wool crepe draw the eye to her girlishly slender waist and hips. The fitted brown wool crepe skirt is lined in pale pink chiffon. Accessories include mid-length cocoa gloves, bracelet, earrings, a fabulous matching headpiece, hose, brown "suede" shoes and purse.

Mel Odom: "I love "Press Conference" because the clothes are so real looking and because of the colors – the peach and brown."

Dolly Cipolla: "There were no changes from the prototype for 'Press Conference' except the gloves were originally gauntlet. The top was a peach and chocolate brown thick woven pique which hugged her so tight. I was thrilled with the purse. I worried about the jewelry, but they (the factory workers) got that, too. When I have the opportunity I like to do it all – from earrings to other jewelry, to shoes."

"Poolside"
     1999 Costume
     Designed by Vince Nowell
     Item #76078
     Original price $34.95
     Ca 1954 film
     Story:
       Three adventurous working girls in "Love for Sail" pool their funds, leave New York and head for the French Riviera. Lounging by the ship's pool, Gene suddenly regales her her chums by doing a little impersonation of the ship's handsome young captain. Borrowing a waiter's tip tray to use as a clipboard, she mimics his officious manner. However, when her friends suddenly become sober, Gene glances over her shoulder. "Captain Right" has been standing behind her the whole time. But hearing Gene go overboard about his many "charms" has made him (secretly) determined to win her heart. Embarrassed, Gene flops back onto her deck chair and throws her beach coat over her head.

      "Poolside" is a sweetheart-neckline sun suit with matching beach coat, circa 1954. In white cotton peppered with a confetti of color, the sun halter top ties at the back of the neck. Attached shorts are pleated both in front and in back. The matching beach coat is lined in sunny yellow, with yellow highlight "cuffs" and pocket flaps. The beach coat sports five different colored buttons – a motif that carries over into *Gene's* button bracelet and the button that adorns each of the ensemble's toe-strap shoes. Green-lensed '50s sunglasses top off the costume.

      Vince Nowell: "This went through a complete makeover from the original concept. The original one, called 'Patio Party,' was originally a one-piece swimsuit with an aqua floral patterned skirt that buttoned down the front. Joan and Frank wanted more color, and Frank found the confetti print. Joan requested that the skirt be changed to a jacket, since they already had a similar skirt in 'Song of Spain.' Although my original design went through several changes, I love the outcome. Those wonderful playsuits of the 40s were my initial inspiration."

      Mel Odom: "'Poolside' is charming and looks adorable on the doll. It was my favorite photo to take for the catalog this year…we were doing things to feature motion to be able to utilize that knee joint really well, and to make it fun."

Opposite Page:
"Picnic in the Country"
1999 Costume
Designed by Lynne Day
Item #76077
Original price $39.95
Period ca 1946
Story:

It was a perfect, sunny July afternoon when Gene and her girlfriend escaped the hectic pace of Hollywood and took a drive in her blue convertible roadster. They stopped at a small farmstand nestled in the cool, inviting shade of two peach trees for some homegrown fruit. The farmstand was a faded wooden shack, but every possible nook was brimming with ripe, succulent fruit, wax-sealed mason jars of homemade preserves, dripping honeycomb. Garden-fresh vegetables, and colorful bunches of dried wildflowers and fragrant herbs. They struck up a lively conversation with the cheery farmer's wife while picking out homebaked bread, jam, peaches and dark red cherries for an impromptu picnic in the country. As they drove off, the farm woman began a new sign "MacKenzie's Fresh Farmstand... Gene Marshall's Favorite Picnic Store!"

"Picnic in the Country" is a day dress circa 1946. The sleeveless dress features a fitted bodice in a red and white gingham check with a pleated panel, boat collar, and white silk lining. The dress extends into an attached box pleat skirt of white waffle cotton blend fabric and a ¼" checked trim at the hem. The matching bolero jacket is fully lined, and features red and white gingham check piping, and a band and tie. Accessories include a matching "band" style hat, shoes, hose, a bracelet, pin, earrings and hat accented with "cherry" bead jewelry.

Mel Odom: "This is *Gene's* first pleated skirt. We've had pleats before, but not all around the skirt. I always love it when we do something new, technique wise, and it looks good."

"Bridge Club"
1999 Costume
Designed by Vince Nowell
Item #76069
Original price $34.95
Ca 1954
Story:

1954's film "Bridge Club" brought Gene back to romantic comedy. In the film, Gene's mother's weekly bridge club is more interested in shuffling hearts than dealing cards. When one of the players gets an "unexpected malady," mother presses Gene into service to fill the empty chair. With Gene as a captive audience, the mothers go to work. One of them has an available (well-to-do) son who would be just perfect for Gene. Could they set up a date? Distracted by her bidding, Gene nods, although her thoughts are on the man of her dreams, a talented (and not-so-well-to-do) writer. Four of the '30s favorite actresses were talked out of retirement by Gene to play the roles of mother and friends. It thrilled movie-goers and restarted the careers of four very happy not-to-be-forgotten film stars.

"Bridge Club" is a classic sheath dress in blue gingham, with a hemline that hits just below the knee. The modest "boat" neckline. Offset by a bow of matching fabric, dips dramatically in the back. White accents come from the cotton belt, flowered picture hat with veil, and open toe slingbacks. The handbag is made from the same material as *Gene's* hat, with a bow and lining of the dress's blue gingham. "Pearl" earrings, necklace, bracelet and wrist-length white gloves complete *Gene's* "Bridge Club" costume.

Vince Nowell: "This outfit (was based) on a day dress called 'Society Luncheon' that I made for *Gene* group members. It was peach gingham with a straw hat with peach blossoms. Last April our *Gene* group took Joan Greene out to dinner. Later she called me up and said 'I love that dress and want it in the line next year.' I did it in peach and another color variation – the lavender blue which Mel loved. I was glad they differentiated from the peach that the *Gene* club members had. The original was a late 40s ensemble and was more mid calf. For 'Bridge Club' the hemline was lifted for the 50s."

Mel Odom: "This is another outfit that looks great with the knee joint. It's just very simple, very tailored."

"Avant Garde"
       1999b Costume
       Designed by José Ferrand
       Item #76085
       Original price $39.95
       Ca 1954
       Story:

       The Avant Garde Gallery was crammed with the elite of the art world for the opening night of their new exhibit. However, Gene's choice of attire was a work of art in itself. The sleeves that floated above her elbows seemed to defy gravity. Gene sipped a glass of champagne. Since she painted as a hobby, the works of art that surrounded her made her eager to leave the party and get back to her own easel. She culd imagine her own works framed on a gallery wall.

       Speaking of frames – there was a large empty frame fixed against the wall with a sign that read "Best in Show." Apparently, this was where the prize winning entry in the exhibition would soon be displayed. She heard someone call "Over here, Miss Marshall!" and turned, framed in the frame, just as the reporter's flash went off. "Perfect!" said the reporter. "That's what I really call the 'Best in Show'!"

Unique "floating sleeves" make this stylish cocktail dress totally "Avant Garde," circa 1956. The carnation pink sleeveless dress features a fitted bodice, decorated with four black buttons. Deeply darted, the bodice tapers sharply to the waist, where the skirt blossoms from beneath. The skirt's fullness is supported by petticoats of shocking pink tulle. Matching armbands that "float" above the elbows serve as sleeves, giving the enitre ensemble a futuristic look, a popular theme in the '50s. A cap-style hat with black bow trim, black bear earrings and necklace, black lace gloves and heels complete the outfit.

Mel Odom: "This was a fashion magazine cover – *Vogue* or *Harper's Bazaar* – with those little detached sleeves. I asked Jose to interpret it. We didn't know what color it was or what the skirt did – it was a close-up in black and white. I just loved those detachable sleeves or cuffs – they looked kind of like Tinkerbell wings! It's something I've never seen done for dolls – it's that new ground that is always exciting to me."

Jose Ferrand: "'Avant Garde' was a request from Mel. The pictures he sent me were only from the waist up. I had the idea of (making it) a cocktail dress, which was so popular in the late 40's. It's a wonderfully inventive design that brings the rare combination of being cute and very mature-looking at the same time. It is basically a cotton strapless dress with those detachable sleeves. The sleeves are totally separate – they sort of snap on."

"Cognac Evening"
    1999 Costume
    Designed by José Ferrand
    Item #76086
    Original price $44.95
    Ca 1951
    Story:
        During visits back home in Cos Cob, Gene was always happy to accept an invitation to enjoy a reception at the Governor's Mansion. As one of Connecticut's most famous 'children,' she attended on the arm of the state representative from her district. She was the perfect guest: listening intently as others spoke and regaling the party with stories of the lighter side of film making. Later, as others settled to enjoy cognac, cigars and tea in the library, Gene excused herself. As she started to leave, the Governor warmly took her gloved hand in his own. 'Gene,' he said, 'you've added just the right touch to the gathering. You are truly one of Connecticut's finest exports.' Gene felt her eyes start to get misty. For even though she was the toast of Hollywood, at heart she was still little Katie Marshall from Cos Cob – and tonight that's exactly who she wanted to be."

"Cognac Evening" is a classic faux two-piece cocktail dress made of tobacco iridescent taffeta. The short-sleeved, collarless bodice features a peplum at the waist. The narrow skirt is provocatively slit in the front. A beaded side panel made of the same taffeta cascades from the left hip, adding movement to the dress. Topping everything off is a unique feathered cap-style hat with brown metallic organza bow at the back. Included are *Gene's* matching purse, decorated with amber beads, amber earrings and matching necklace, black opera-length gloves, and ribbon cloth-covered shoes in brown.

Jose Ferrand: "'Cognac Evening' was the first costume I designed for *Gene*. I had started it as a companion for Timothy Albert's 'El Morocco,' even before I met Mel. It was one of the original designs I showed Mel and he and Joan loved it from the start. I don't know what my inspiration was, I just sketched and sketched, and I happened to have this cognac iridescent taffeta at home. The original hat was more of a faceted covered cap, etched with beads with black netting, veiling the eyes, and cognac marabou feathers on one side."

Mel Odom: "This is devastating – drop dead gorgeous. It is one of the most beautiful doll dresses I have ever seen in my life. Joan came up with the hat, got someone to design it with the beautiful little feathers."

Joan Greene: "José designed on 7th Avenue for a number of years and his specialty was designing cocktail suits. 'Cognac Evening' is a fabulous example of Jose's work."

"Honeymoon"
> **1999 Costume**
> **Designed by José Ferrand**
> **Item #93524**
> **Original price $44.95**
> **Ca 1950**
> **Story:**

"What would mother and daddy think?"

Gene Marshall studied herself in the dressing room mirror. In a few minutes she would be under the hot lights filming the final scene of "Monaco." Rubbing her arms and drawing the diaphanous folds of lace around her, she would step off the balcony and back into the honeymoon suite – just in time for the Prince, her new husband, to hand her a bubbly glass of champagne. A toast, a passionate kiss, and then... Fade Out.

This dazzling peignoir set would be just perfect for the moment. Her thoughts turned to her parents and the pajamas they dressed her in for bed: footies on to keep her toes warm and back flap securely buttoned, they would give her her teddy and scoot her off to bed with a kiss. Picking up the same teddy bear she tried to imagine little Katie toddling up to bed in Cos Cob wearing blue lace and silk. Giggling at the thought, she walked through her dressing room door and onto the set.

"Honeymoon" is a classic peignoir/nightgown set, circa 1950. The full-length nightgown is of a sky blue silk charmeuse, fitted close at the hips and flaring bell-like to the floor. The panel of peek-a-boo lace is inset in the front. The bust is accentuated with shirred tulle and iridescent blue beads. Shirred tulle and iridescent blue beads also adorn the matching lace peignoir. The peignoir is a long-sleeved bolero-shaped top spilling into a floor-length lace train, lined in organza and trimmed at the hem to match the bodice. Included are *Gene's* "aquamarine" earrings, light blue "fur"-trimmed mules and a light blue hair ribbon.

Jose Ferrand: "'Honeymoon' dervieved from one of the costumes I first showed Mel and Joan. It was an evening dress of black pontiff prenetting over a nude lining with a full gathered skirt. Joan felt that *Gene* had many evening dresses and that doll collectors love the lingerie look. I changed it. The gown metamorphosed into a negligee and peignoir that barely resemble the predicessor. Without the peignoir, the negligee is sexy, yet refined. With the pegnoir on, the neckline almost has an 18th century flavor, increased by the Watteau-like back trailing into a train. There seemed to be a thousand French seams and many hours of hand-beading on the original prototype. I wondered how on earth they would be able to mass-produce it, but somehow they have done it and done it beautifully."

Mel Odom: "This is based on an evening gown that Joan could see as lingerie. Jose used the same basic design of the bodice as the evening gown and made this whole pegnoir set around it. The little ruffled hemline is toile and beads. The beads give it a little bit of weight so that it hangs lovely. When Joan said 'I see it as lingerie,' I'm like, 'I think you're crazy, but be my guest.' But it is beautiful."

Opposite Page:
"Sunday Afternoon"
    1999 Costume
    Designed by Abigail Haskell,
      a winner of the Young
      Designers of America
      Competition
    Item #93521
    Original price $39.95
    Ca 1953
    Story:

The film "Rain Song" wrapped for the weekend and Gene was taking a Sunday stroll by the New England seaside. Walking along the wharf, she stopped at a small stand that sold souvenirs. The grizzled salt who ran the stand was deftly assembling a ship-in-a-bottle when Gene walked in. ""cuse me, Miss – but don't I know you?" he said.

Gene blushed, "I don't think so, captain. My name is Katie I'm from Cos Cob..."

"Been a lot of places but I never been there," the captain said. Then he snapped his fingers, "Of course – you look like that pretty movie star, Miss Gene Marshall, She's one of my favorites. You're pretty enough to be a movie star yourself! Didja ever think of going out to Hollywood and getting in moving pictures?"

"Gene's eyes sparkled. "All the time, sir. And thank you for the complement. And by the way, that's a lovely ship-in-a-bottle – is it for sale?"

"Sunday Afternoon" is a two-piece spring ensemble of a sleeveless sheath and a tailored jacket, circa 1953. The navy blue sleeveless rayon sheath is peppered with white polka dots and has a square neckline. The long-sleeved white waist-length jacket accented with matching blue and white polka dot trim at the sleeves and collar. Accessories include the wide-brimmed hat, trimmed with a red silk poppy and a "pearl" and navy bead hat pin, "pearl" earrings and necklace, white wicker purse, and white open-toed slingbacks.

Mel Odom: "One of the things I like most about 'Sunday Afternoon' is that it is a very demure looking suit, very Sunday School looking, until you take the jacket off and then there is a Marilyn Monroe dress – a sexy little sheath – a very different animal!"

"Black Ribbon"
    1999 Costume
    Designed by Tim Kennedy
    Item #76088
    Original price $39.95
    Story:

Gene plays the part of Gilda Webster in "The Black Ribbon," a young widow who suddenly learns that her husband has left her penniless. For playing an older woman in a role that called for her to run the gamut of emotions, Gene won the Golden Star Award as Best Actress. In the film, after hearing about her financial state, a distraught Gilda falls into a fitful sleep. She dreams that she is dressed in black, running through a cemetery. Suddenly a light pierces the darkness. As she hurries toward it, she hears a voice calling to her. It is the voice of Jeremy Watts, the handsome attorney handling her case. She runs into his protective embrace as bells start to ring.

Bells ringing—the phone! It's Jeremy calling with the news that the Times-Journal is looking for a fashion writer. Would Gilda mind if he made her an appointment with the editor...?"

"Black Ribbon" is a close-fitting charmeuse sheath, with a sweetheart neckline. Its basic black is relieved by a hidden lining of mauve, circa 1949. A long-sleeved overdress of black netting, tapered at the waist, is set off dramatically by insets of horizontal satin ribbons, giving a black-on-black effect to the sheath. A rhinestone horseshoe shaped brooch adds a touch of sparkle to the ensemble. *Gene* carries an iridescent black feather and black satin ribbon fan. The ensemble includes a veiled crownless woven hat with hatpin, rhinestone post earrings, black heels, black net gloves, and black hose.

Tim Kennedy: "This interprets a dress that Marlene Dietrich wore in a black and white movie. Mel saw it and said he would love to have *Gene* wear something like that someday. Marlene Dietrich's wore a very different hat, a hat with flowers. I wanted to play up the mandarin feeling of the collar with this hat. And used the accessories to play up the sheerness of the fabric. The feather fan is a concession to Orry-Kelly*, who had a tendency to make extravagant designs. I love "Black Ribbon' with the jacket off – the jacket is almost a piece of sculpture." (* Orrey-Kelly designed the women's clothes for the films "Maltese Falcon," "Casablanca," "Some Like it Hot," and won the Oscar for "Les Girls.")

"Somewhere Summer"
 1999 Costume
 Designed by Tim Kennedy
 Item #93522
 Original price $44.95
 Ca 1952
 Story:

The weather outside the theatre is frightful – winter at its worst. But once inside there is the imagined scent of sweet summer blossoms. Gene's latest hit "Somewhere Summer" is nearing its end. There, on screen, is Gene, standing in a beautiful rose garden. A soft breeze ruffles her dotted dress as she waits. Will he be there to keep his promise to sweep her away to where it's somewhere summer? A drop of rain falls, and then another. Soon a chilling rain engulfs the garden—and Gene. She turns to leave the garden, blinded by the rain and her tears. Suddenly she hears the sound of running feet and her name being shouted. She stops and turns. There he is. She rushes to him through the downpour. As his arms encircle her, she smiles through her tears. For it is then she realizes that, no matter what the weather is outside, when you find true love, the place that's "Somewhere Summer" is always in your heart.

"Somewhere Summer" is a crisp white dress of dotted organza, layered over cool white taffeta, circa 1952. The underbodice features a sweet heart neckline. The dress features dramatic "lantern" sleeves, with the waist defined by a black velvet ribbon into which a brilliant red rose is tucked. A full skirt flares dramatically from the fitted waist. It is given body by a tulle petticoat trimmed in black stitching. *Gene's* face is framed by a large sheer white hat trimmed in black ribbon. Included are white "pearl" earrings and necklace, short white gloves, black shoes and seamed hoisery.

Tim Kennedy: "This was one of my own ideas. It was inspired by those ethereal chiffon garden party dresses of the 1930s, with a horsehair hat, but updated to *Gene's* time. It is very feminine."

Mel Odom: "'Somewhere Summer' Timmy just made up on his own, completely out of the blue. He brought it over and I flipped over it. I wanted it for my own collection, but Joan saw it and loved it and it went in the line immediately. Timmy describes this outfit as saying 'I'm sweet, damn it!'"

"Sunset Celebration"
1999 Costume
Designed by Vince Nowell
Item #76076
Original Price $39.95
Story:

"It's just another day," Gene kept repeating to herself. It was her birthday, but no one had acknowledged it. On the set, it was business as usual on this balmy April 17th. Finally, the director called out, "Okay, people—that's it for today." Slowly Gene made her way to her dressing trailer. At her trailer door... a box-- a costume sample from a designer friend. 'Give this a test run; for me , would you, Darling?' said the note. Gene slipped into the sunset-hued gown. Already her mood brightened. Then – a knock. It was Eddie, from the crew. 'I was over at Studio A and well, there's something you just gotta see, Miss Marshall,' he said. 'Don't change. Just come like you are.'

Gene followed Eddie to an empty sound stage, and as he pushed aside the heavy doors, Gene was suddenly caught in the the warmth of crew, cast and friends—all there for Gene's birthday. And as the sun set, one of Hollywood's brightest stars celebrated something more than 'just another day.'"

Fashioned from orange dupioni silk, "Sunset Celebration" has a snuggly fitted bodice (with a sweetheart neckline) that flares to a full skirt, covering tulle petticoats in contrasting shades. Circa 1955. It sports a diagonal sash of rose and saffron satin, jeweled at the bodice and tucked beneath the silk belt, where it flares to the hemline. The matching clutch is made of the same three colored dress fabrics and is studded with a jeweled snap. *Gene's* jewelry is beaded in matching sunset tones and includes earrings, necklace and bracelet. Her ribboned shoes make up the final tri-colored accent to this lovely outfit.

Mel Odom: "'Sunset Celebration' has my favorite colors – it's very beautiful. I love the fabric and the silhouette is wonderful."

Opposite Page:
"Secret Sleuth"
1999 Costume
Designed by Tim Kennedy,
**   based on an authentic period design from Valentino's in Hollywood, CA**
Item #93523
Original price $39.95
Story:

Quick! It appears the game's afoot! And in "Montage," a 1948 mystery set in the world of art and artifice, things are not always what they appear to be. In the film, Gene's father, a world-renowned artist, is missing. The key to his disappearance appears to be a seemingly innocent portrait painted by her father. Having narrowly escaped a confrontation with a mysterious figure in the shadowy street of old Rome, Gene dons her most Sherlock Holmes-ian outfit and heads to the gallery. As the bidding for her father's painting begins, the flash of Gene's yellow glove cuts through the air. Who will own the painting at the evening's end? That shouldn't be a secret to any sleuth!

"Secret Sleuth" is a simple, long-sleeved black crepe sheath topped by a short black and white plaid woven wool cape, lined in the same material. Circa 1948. The dress features patch pockets in the same fabric as *Gene's* cape. A yellow scarf tied at the neck and yellow wrist-length gloves bring a splash of color to the ensemble. *Gene* sports a black and white checked beret and carries a black box purse with gold closure. The ensemble includes black button earrings, black open-toed sling backs, and hose.

Tim Kennedy: "This outfit I absolutely adore! On one of her trips to New York, Joan Greene brought in a garment rented from Valentino's, a Hollywood costume shop, made by a Hollywood designer in the 1940s. I did quick sketches and made a faithful interpretation. I didn't remember the construction of the bodice, so I reconfigured the darts so that the buttons would make sense. The buttonholes were strange and hard to do. They were like a half-opened eye shape hole in the fabric, with no stitching or binding, but diagonal to follow the line of the cape. The original garment's pocket piece, although it had real buttonholes, did not function, it was a decorative applique. I offered Mel a series of suggestions about accessories, and the chrome yellow was the perfect accent color."

Mel Odom: "This was an original garment that Joan acquired from a costume rental shop in Hollywood. We loved the buttoning action on it, the cape attaching and detaching. Timmy did a very literal interpretation of the garment, but he changed the way it was constructed – simplified things to minimize bulk. If you over-produce a garment, you can have an authentic potholder! Timmy also came up with mustard yellow gloves and scarf which is a cinematic thing – to attract you to her hands and face."

"Breathless"
    1999 Retailer Exclusive Doll
    Designed by Stephanie
      Bruner, a winner in the
      Young Designers of America
      Competition
    Item #76074
    Original price $99.95
    Story:

It was a magical California evening: the Hollywood Roosevelt Hotel was ablaze with lights from dazzling crystal chandeliers, spotlights, flashbulbs, and Hollywood's brightest luminaries celebrating mogul producer Eric von Sternberg's 55th birthday.

The cub reporter stood alone outside the front door, fiddling with his camera. The flash hadn't worked all evening and he thought about how furious his editor was going to be with no photos from the party of the year. He might even loose his job!

A sleek, white limo purred up to the re-carpeted stairs and Gene Marshall stepped out and hurried up the stairs. Gene's celestial blue gown glimmered in the moonlight, softly reflecting on lustrous pearls, satin and gleaming gold. Her shawl floasted behind her as diaphanous as a heavenly cloud swept with golden stars. Her face lifted skyward and he caught his breath as such inexpressible beauty. He readied his camera and called, "How are you tonight, Miss Marshall?" "Breathless!" she laughingly replied, kindly pausing to pose. Miraculously, the flash popped! "Breathless" was the morning edition's headline under her photo. To the cub reporter, Gene was the angel who saved his career.

"Breathless" is a strapless evening gown of celestial blue satin. Circa 1956. It is hand-embellished with golden beads, stars, "pearls" and golden metallic embroidery in an intricate mixed pattern. The bodice features a princess waist and sweetheart neckline. The full skirt is uniquely accented with a reverse pleat in back, lined in gold lamé. The outfit includes a beaded azure shawl, "pearl" necklace and earrings, golden mesh shoes, hose and a double-flounced lace crinoline. *Gene's* full, champagne-blonde curls are parted on the side with an enchanting forehead wave.

Mel Odom: "This is a student design that was originally done in cream and we did it in a pale blue. I love that sort of Jean Harlow hairdo going on."

Joan Greene: "I love the star burst pattern on the skirt. I think of it as fireworks on a soft evening sky."

"At Home for the Holidays"
    1999 Retailer Exclusive Costume, LE 9,999
    Designed by Tim Kennedy
    Item #76084
    Original price $49.95
    Story:

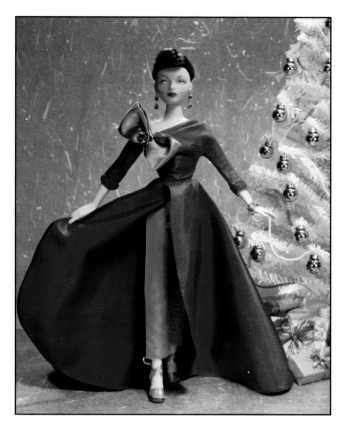

    This holiday travel to sunny California as Gene Marshall invites the country to join her "At Home for the Holidays!" The cast and crew from NBS's "Holiday Magic" became a second family to Gene during the creation of last year's special. Now most have them have flown to the West Coast to work on what may become an annual Gene Marshall holiday event. As cameras, lights and sound equipment fill her home, Gene plans a few surprises to make this holiday one that will always be remembered. Always thoughtful, Gene has taken special care to put up the fashionable white flocked Christmas tree given to her by the producer and crew the year before. As the final notes of the final song fade over the airwaves, Gene steps away from the tree – revealing hand-picked, hand-wrapped presents for each member of the cast and crew. Every day's a holiday when you're a friend of Gene Marshall's!

    Gene is "At Home for the Holidays" in this cocktail-style hostess outfit with luxurious overskirt. Circa 1957. The top is made of an iridescent taffeta of lavender and ruby, the Capri-style pants are of lavender satin Long sleeves (gathered above the wrist) emerge from the angled neckline of the fitted bodice. The daring neckline ends in a lavender bow accented by the multi-colored brooch. The ensemble includes lavender lace-ups, multi-stone bracelet and "ruby and gold" drop earrings.

Tim Kennedy: "This was based on a stylized illustration of an evening gown, but a great deal of liberty was taken in interpreting it. Joan Green wanted a hostess outfit. We used the dramatic asymmetry in front and made the overskirt move into the bodice design. The colors were dictated by the fabric, a changeable taffeta. I found a satin to mirror the lighter color in the taffeta."

Mel Odom: "I've always loved those lounge costumes with pants and an overskirt. Timmy always does things that aren't the most obvious color solutions – this has the colors of fuschia blossoms."

"At Home for the Holidays—Take Two"
    1999 Commemorative Doll, LE 10
    Designed by Tim Kennedy
    This is certified as one of ten *Gene* dolls dressed especially for the 1999 *Gene* Signing Tour. It represents one of the costume tests for *Gene's* 1957 Christmas television spectacular, broadcast coast-to-coast in compatible color. Although *Gene* adored the dress, the lighting technician assured her that its beautiful hues would not read well on color sets across the country. The costume is based the 1999 Retailer Exclusive Costume "At Home for the Holidays." Frank Rotundo managed the developmental changes for this limited edition.

Tim Kennedy: "The color here is hard to describe, the changeable taffeta is black with peacock blue highlights that looks like a dark midnight blue. The accent color is a light lavender, less pink that the other version."

"Tea Time"
    1999 FAO Schwarz Exclusive
     Doll
    Designed by Lynne Day
    Original Price $100
    Story:

"She was a famous – many would say infamous—columnist, notorious for ferreting out scandal, backbiting gossip and tattling rumors. Hers was a formidable name in Hollywood, with the power of a million avid readers behind her. One word in her weekly column – a subtle insinuation or a catty opinion – could spell disaster for a career. Movie stars dreaded interviews with her. That's why the gossip columnist was surprised to receive an invitation from Gene Marshall inviting her to tea at the Plaza hotel in New York. Gene has just won a Golden Star for her role in "The Black Ribbon," and the gossip columnist jumped at the chance to dig up some exclusive dirt on this new star.

Gene was waiting for her amid the Grecian columns, flowers and exquisite settings of crystal, silver, china and linen at the Plaza's High Tea. From the first, the gossip columnist found herself disarmed by the genuine warmth of Gene's welcoming smile. She mentally awarded Gene points for her impeccable ensemble and thoughtful conversation. Gene was so candid, so amiable, that before the notorious gossip columnist knew it, they were chatting like dear friends. She even confided to Gene her dreams for writing a cookbook. When they finally parted—Gene to meet her family for dinner, and the gossip columnist to write a glowing report – they both cherished the feeling that an abiding friendship was born over tea at the Plaza.

"Tea Time" is one of *Gene's* favorite interview dresses, presenting a picture of tailored elegance, circa 1943. The long sleeved, collarless dress is a classically tailored "A" line of navy blue georgette lined in silk. White soutache braid accents the neckline, shoulders and hips. The hat is a matching headband topped with three upright navy and white ribbons of charmease and organza. The two-toned "leather" shoes are in the "spectator" pump style. The outfit includes a "leather" clutch purse, hose, and "pearl" earrings and bracelet.

Lynne Day: " This dress had drastic changes made in color. Originally it was stronger, more vivid – a different kind of outfit. When it was switched to navy blue, it clicked since the emphasis was on the 1940s. I loved it when it became sober navy. The wartime restrictions limited the yards of fabric. To keep spirits up women used hats, gloves and purses as accents. They would recycle old trims to make a hat or dress look new."

Mel Odom: "This is based on a fashion drawing that I loved. I love tailored little dresses like that. I love the braiding on it and it's got a great hat. The outfit is very real looking. Notice that the shoes are full leatherette spectator pumps – I think maybe they're the first full shoes we've done for *Gene*."

"On the Veranda"
   1999 Parkwest Spring Exclusive
   Costume
   Designed by Lynne Day
   Item # 76071
   Original price $49.95
   Story:
   Gene is the guest of honor at an afternoon fete hosted by an internationally renowned Italian director. The lavish hors d'oeuvres, champagne, music, dancing and the breathtaking view of the fabulous gardens from the veranda, are all part of his elaborate Machiavellian plot to woo the talented American movie actress into staying in Italy and starring in his next film. He had seen a number of her pictures, and was highly impressed by her talent. His intuition – that innate sense that made him such a brilliant director – whispered to him that their collaboration would be electrifying, all but ensuring the movie's success. She was a prize to be won, so he spent long hours devising this subtle campaign to win her.

But at his first sight of Gene Marshall in person, all his motives, all his carefully phrased and well-rehearsed words of persuasion flew completely out of his mind. He was entranced by her loveliness, intelligence and sweet charm. Gene danced as delicately as a butterfly in his arms, her light floral scent teasing his senses into dreamy bliss. Gene spoke wistfully of home, and her worries that her next movie "Bitter Snow" was still missing a director. Late that evening, as they stood alone together on the veranda, he eagerly agreed to come with gene to direct "Bitter Snow"...which had been Gene's hope all along.

"On the Veranda" is a romantic tea-length peach dress, circa 1955. The silk underdress has a strapless sweetheart neckline softly overlaid by a sheer veiling of peach organza. Full gathered translucent sleeves and a satin Peter Pan collar accented with a leafy flower lends a delicate, ladylike beauty to the ensemble. The silk and organza skirt blooms with silk flowers over a full crinoline of peach tulle. A sweeping satin bow and sash prettily accent the back. A matching picture hat, lace-up satin shoes and "pearl" earrings complete the outfit.

Lynne Day: "I was asked to design a big, fluffy dress and maybe put flowers on it. My idea for 'On the Veranda' was inspired by Grace Kelly's bridesmaid dresses which had little Peter Pan collars with the big organza dress and scattered flowers on the skirt."

Mel Odom: "This is really beautiful. It's very faux Southern belle. I had an experience in Rosemont with this particular outfit. Mary Costa, who was the voice of Sleeping Beauty in Disney's film, was there. I loved 'Sleeping Beauty' when I was little, so I stood in line to meet her. When she saw my badge and realized I was *Gene's* creator, she just went off on *Gene*. I ran back to the booth and said 'please, you have to give me something that I can give to Mary Costa—she was just so wonderful!' They gave me a blonde doll with 'On the Veranda' and I ran back and gave it to her. She said. 'I can't believe you gave me this one, it's exactly like the costume I wore in (an opera). I had long blonde hair and this doll does not look unlike me in that opera – it's amazing.' She was a child again when she opened the box and saw that doll. I will always love this outfit because of that experience."

141

Unforgettable
1999 Ashton-Drake Exclusive Doll
Designed by Dolly Cipolla
Item #76075
Original price $99.95
Story:

New York City has always held a soft spot in its worldly heart for Gene Marshall – after all, she was discovered there. So New York was thrilled when Gene came "home" to film "Personal Secretary" in Manhattan. When the night of the premiere came, massive spotlights swept the sky outside the same movie theatre that Gene once worked as an usherette. The excitedly buzzing crowd were held back by velvet-roped stanchions, while mounted police stood by. A platinum silver limousine purred to a stop at the head of the red carpet, and out stepped Gene. She uncurled from the limo wearing a sultry mermaid gown of rich dubonnet wine that lovingly graced every contour. Her platinum hair shone like sterling silver in the flashbulbs. With hundreds of fans cheering her, Mom and Dad in the front row, and lavish bouquets in her hotel suite from four well-known leading men...the night was unforgettable for both Gene and New York.

"Unforgettable" is an innovative daring evening gown. Its rich wine hue, called dubonnet, was a popular fashion color in its time, circa 1957. The gown hugs every contour until it flares in a rounded petal "mermaid"-style cut, accented with a bow behind the knee. The costume is fully lined in pale pink silk. The flare includes six layers of dubonnet and mauve tulle, with rose "crystal" beadwork. The outfit includes a mauve lace scarf, evening gloves, "amethyst" and "diamond" necklace and bracelet, drop "diamond" earrings, hose, and matching shoes. *Gene's* platinum hair is swept back and curled under for a sleek, silvery leonine look.

Mel Odom: "I think 'Unforgettable' is one of the most drop-dead glamorous things we've ever done for *Gene*. The wine color on the platinum blond *Gene* – it's very Monroe looking."

Joan Greene: "'Unforgettable' is based on a photograph that Mel and I found and just loved. The original dress was probably in velvet, but in working with Dolly we felt it would be better in this raw silk look. This is the first *Gene* in platinum hair- sort of like Carol Lombard. Although Lombard was more of a 1930's star, it would have carried over and has that kind of feeling."

Dolly Cipolla: "The prototype and the final gown are really different – it changed color four times! The tulle was working but we struggled with the lining color. At first it was gold. Joan said 'if all else fails, choose pink.' The hourglass shape has so many panels that it was made not to have an underskirt. It slips smooth over her waist, almost like a girdle. Ashton-Drake wanted a big statement – a wild gown."

An American Countess
1999 Parkwest/NALED
Exclusive Doll, LE 7,500
Designed by Christine D. Curtis
Item #76082
Original Price $99.95
Story:

In 1952's "Royal Rebel," the tale of a Broadway star who marries "above her station"—the down-to-earth heir to the throne of a small duchy—Gene shown like the diamonds in her tiara. At first the citizens of the land rebuff Gene as an American gold-digger. Only the palace servants accept her, as mistress of the castle – and as a friend. With the servant's help, Gene concocts a plan. On the last evening of the annual Harvest festival, Gene suddenly appears at the top of the staircase wearing the dress worn by the duchy's beloved Countess Cornelia many years before and the jewels presented to Cornelia on an American good will tour.

As she descends the staircase, Gene begins singing "A Promise for Tomorrow" – a song from her most popular Broadway show. Touched by the inspiring lyrics and the heartfelt emotions behind them, the citizens realize she truly cares about her adopted country. And, one by one, they bow to their beloved new Countess.

"An American Countess" is a grand ballgown fashioned of fuchsia taffeta. Its daring bodice features off-the-shoulder organza sleeves covered in sequins. The sequin and metallic embroidery continues down the organza bodice onto a front panel, forming a stemmed flower pattern. The spangle embroidery extends to a full overskirt supported by a tulle petticoat. Includes a clutch in matching fuchsia with a gold chain handle, "diamond" earrings and multi-strand pendant necklace. Fuchsia ribbon-tie shoes complete the ensemble. *Gene's* dark brown hair is crowned by a "diamond" tiara.

Mel Odom: "The original had an enormous skirt, but that was brought down to a smaller scale."

Joan Greene: Some of *Gene's* costumes "have increased the skill level of the workers in the factories. You have people sitting there doing hand ribbon embroidery, and hand-sewing on every sequin when they were used to gluing. We have carried forward some of the skills that the people in the 1940s and 50s knew how to do that are almost a lost art today because of the way we all live."

"Priceless"
FAO Schwarz Exclusive Doll
Designed by José Ferrand
Original Price $110.
Story:

"The rumor mill was in a frenzy. Reports were flying around that Gene Marshall had consented to model a necklace in an advertisement for one of the world's most prestigious jewelry houses. Excited fans clustered around the jeweler's on the rumored night. Velvet ropes blocked off the front of the store – a promising sign. And then...suddenly, there she stands, poised and regal, draped in diamonds. But the most dazzling gemstone can't hold a carat to the fire and sparkle provided by Gene Marshall.

And then it's over. The photographer takes apart his camera. The lights are turned off and the precious jewels are carried away by security guards. And now, Gene gets to relish the moment – with her fans that crowded to catch a glimpse of their favorite star. One of the policemen has thrown his coat over Gene's shoulders to protect her from the evening's chill. There she stands, laughing happily with the people she makes her movies for; signing autographs and trading stories. It's then that Gene once again knows the devotion of her fans is really the most priceless treasure of all.

"Priceless" is a dramatically beautiful strapless sheath evening gown of inky black silk velvet, lined in pink, circa 1949. The two large satin "lapels" sweep downward from the sheath's waist to hem, crossing over the front v-slit. Two touches are truly priceless: the stunning "diamond" necklace *Gene* is modeling, made up of three rows of rhinestones; and the 22-inch long white faux fur stole, lined in white satin. The ensemble includes rhinestone cluster earrings, black evening gloves, black hosery and black satin strap shoes. *Gene's* hair is a beautiful sunset red, brushed back in tousled, soft curls.

Mel Odom: "'Priceless' is one of the most ultra glamorous things we have ever done for *Gene*. I love that shade of red that we chose for the hair color. It's another design that I asked Jose to interpret. It's a tuxedo evening gown based on a photograph that we saw. We couldn't tell what the fabrics were or a number of things, but Jose interpreted it for us. He added the 'diamond' buttons and I think a stole. People have been screaming for that shade of red for the hair. We knew that a redhead should wear that outfit – completely black and white and diamonded. It is spectacular – it really is!"

Jose Ferrand: "'Priceless' was a costume that Mel requested me to make. The crisscrossing panels were quite a feat of engineering. All those diamonds and the white fur stole was a wonderfully graphic effect that reminds me of those wonderful illustrations by Grauau. That's one of Mel's favorites, too. At first the hair color made me nervous, but now I think it looks terribly chick."

Accessories

"White Christmas"
Musical White-flocked Christmas Tree that plays *I'm Dreaming of a White Christmas*
Designed by Joan Greene
22-inches tall with wood base ornaments: 24 pink balls and 24 blue balls in storage box
Item #94398 (accessory only)
Original price $44.95
"White Christmas" is *Gene*'s fashionable white-flocked Christmas tree, a gift from the 'Holiday Magic' producer and crew. 21" tall with a musical base that plays "White Christmas." Includes star topper, and our dozen hand-blown glass ornaments in a special gift box. Circa 1956.

"Out for a Stroll"
Designed by Etta Foran
Item #93547 (pair of dogs)
Original price $29.95
Gene's pair of terriers, "Dottie" and "Dashiell," parade on their golden double leash in their matching jeweled collars. They were created for *Gene* especially by Etta Foran.

Gene's Dress Form
Designed by Joan Greene
Item #94390
Original price $19.95
From catalog: "Custom-crafted to *Gene*'s exact measurements and height, so any costume you display on it will look as wonderful as when *Gene* is wearing it herself. Use the forms to create a dramatic display of *Gene*'s entire wardrobe. Black and clear acrylic.

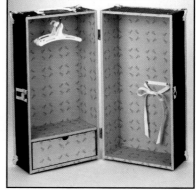

Gene's Wardrobe Trunk
Designed by Joan Greene
Item #93504
Original price $69.95
From catalog: "Designed to store and protect her wardrobe. It's 16" high with a black leatherette surface and a bold, golden 'Gene' star logo on the front."

"Hot Day in Hollywood"
Designed by Joan Greene
Item #93548
Original price $34.95
From catalog: "Here's all *Gene* needs to keep cool at poolside as she reviews some scripts for future production. Five-piece accessory set includes miniature table fan, phone, two miniature movie scripts…and *Gene*'s own rhinestone-studded sunglasses!"

1999 Accessory Packages

Gene's Bedroom Suite:

Gene's Dresser Item #76073 $79.95
Features an elegant swan motif, includes "inlaid" wood panels, exquisite carving, a beautiful mirror and working drawers.

Gene's Swan Bed, Item #76087, $89.95
 This handcrafted sleigh bed features an elegant swan motif, plush mattress and pillows.

"USO Package"
Item #94677
$34.95
A special trunk filled with a 48-star flag, travel stickers, USO sign, microphone, letters from GIs, and miniature "autographed" pin-ups of Gene. (Complements "USO," "Stand UP and Cheer," and "Farewell Golden Moon.")

"Gene's Picnic Basket"
Item #76072
$34.95
Wicker picnic basket with closable lid contains wine glasses, napkins, placemats, dinner plates, salad plates and a metal service (all for two), a serving platter, and a red rose. (Complements "Picnic in the Country.")

"Gene's Birthday Party Set"
Item #76079
$29.95
Confetti, four party hats, four "blow outs," a cake with candles, and card.
(Complements "Sunset Celebration.")

"Gene's Director's Chair"
Item #76080
$29.95
White wooden frame with a canvas seat and back, with Gene's logo on one side and her name on the other.

"Gene's Mirror"
Item #94678
$19.95
Decorative floral trim with a pearlized finish frames a beveled mirror.

"Gene's Patio Set"
Item #94679
$49.95
White "wrought iron" glass-topped table and

two chairs with monogrammed cushions.

"Gene 'Paper' Doll Sets"
Items #92931, #92932, #92933
$12.95 each
Magnetic MagiCloth. Three different sets; includes Gene form and six costumes.

"Jewelry Set"
Item #92938
$34.95
Two complete sets of necklaces, bracelets and earrings.

"Menu for Romance (CD)"
Item #93321
$14.95
Music form the 1940s and 50s, plus two original songs: "She'd Rather Dance" written and performed by Mel Odom, and "Share the Dream" (Gene's Theme).

"Menu for Romance (Video)"
Item #93323
$14.95
Mel Odom performs his original song "She'd Rather Dance," and a collage of 1999 Gene dolls and some of her fans in "Share the Dream."

Fans & Fanfare

The First Gene Convention

The *Gene* doll may be unprecedented in that she was out less than a year before the first convention was planned in her honor. Although *Gene* was not an instant success with the general public, there was a strong support group of collectors on the Internet and people were attracted to her after seeing the first advertisements of the doll.

Benita Schwartz was involved with *Gene* from the first glimpse of "Blue Goddess" in the *Doll Reader* article by Beauregard Houston-Montgomery. Benita had been involved in the doll world since 1982, mainly as an "Alexander fanatic," in her words, so *Gene* was a departure for her. "The doll intrigued me so much," Benita says. She became part of the close-knit group that regularly posted on the *Gene* message board on America Online. From time to time someone would post that it would be fun for the group to meet.

Because Benita had experience in planning conventions, she volunteered to put together a convention for the *Gene* fans. Her background was in math, and she had worked as a credit manager, but since 1994 she had been putting on doll shows under the name F&M Productions.

The first *Gene* convention was held the second weekend of November 1996 in Newark, New Jersey. On Saturday, the group attended workshops; Ashton-Drake contributed an outfit and gave a program on the concept of *Gene*. Nick Hill gave a program on caring for dolls, and Laura Meisner spoke on Hairstyling. There was a hat workshop, a

"Atlantic City Beauty" was the souvenir costume for the first Convention.

teddy/lingerie workshop, and a question and answer period. Although Benita originally planned for 150 people and 110 actually attended, over $10,000 was raised at the auction of one-of-a-kind *Gene* dolls for the Gay Men's Health Crisis.

On Sunday there was the first fashion doll show, which has since become a staple event for other organizations. At that time a lot of people didn't understand the fashion doll concept.

"My Favorite Witch" was the souvenir doll for the 1997 Newark, NJ, convention.

tume party and dancing in addition to the Saturday and Sunday events. This time there was a *Gene* doll as the souvenir, "My Favorite Witch."

In March 1998 a West Coast *Gene* convention was held at the Hollywood Roosevelt Hotel, the location of the first Academy Awards. Organized by the Hollywood *Gene* Fan Club, 250 *Gene* fans gathered for a swing band, a hair workshop, a slide presentation by Ashton-Drake, and autograph sessions with Mel Odom.

For Benita Schwartz's 1998 convention back on the East Coast, the original plans were for 450 collectors. The final count was closer to 750 fans. Because of the turnout, the same kind of activities were planned that were so popular before, but with everyone put into one of three groups. The theme was "Broadway Medley" and the *piece de resistance* a special Broadway live musical performance. The convention souvenir doll "Broadway Medley" wore a dress designed by Tim Kennedy.

In 1999 for the first time other established organizations held events which featured a limited edition *Gene* doll. In April the Santa Fe Doll Art Symposium held a *Gene* breakfast at which the "Santa Fe Celebration" doll was the souvenir. Wearing a dress designed by Vince Nowell, a variation of "Sunset Celebration," in shades of blue and turquoise. At the United Federation of Doll Clubs annual convention in Washington, D.C., in August, a dinner with a theatre troupe entertaining with a murder mystery "Murder on the Set" was a roaring success. The souvenir doll "On the Set" was attired as befitting the convention theme "Elegance and Opulence" in a cream and black lace gown originally designed as a one-of-a-kind for Mel Odom's personal collection by Tim Kennedy.

The theme of Benita's 1999 convention, mid-October in Cherry Hill, New Jersey, is "50's Flashback."

After the first convention, more and more people became attracted to the *Gene* doll. The Online interest was growing and there was a bigger demand for anything related to *Gene*, so Benita volunteered to do a second convention. This one was planned for 250 collectors, plus additional people from Ashton-Drake and the press. It was based on the same concept as the first one, with seminars and workshops for everyone. Since this one was planned for the Halloween weekend, the theme was "Masquerade." On Friday there was a cos-

RIGHT:
"Broadway Medley"
1998 Convention Doll, LE 750?
Designed by Tim Kennedy
Tim Kennedy: "This was designed so that the lines of the skirt followed the lines of the peplum, and the diagonal lines converged at the waist. It was very intentional that the skirt is shorter in the back, and rather subtle. I can just see some starlet coming onstage appearing to be wearing a full-length gown, but when she turns the dress shows her heels in back."

"Santa Fe Celebration"
1999 commemorative doll, LE 250
Designed by Vince Nowell
This special doll was designed to celebrate the simultaneous introduction of "Sunset celebration" into the Gene collection during the International Collector's Exhibition, April 1999. Inspired by the blue Santa Fe sky, this unique combination is a tribute to the glorious Southwest.

Vince Nowell: "This variation was as much a surprise for me as for the people who received it. It was quite an honor to have a doll for a special event, because I only had outfits, not a doll (in the line) this year."

"On the Set"
1999
Commemorative
Doll, LE 350
Designed by Tim
Kennedy
For the United Federation of Doll Clubs Annual Convention, Washington, D.C.

The gown with the black lace strapless top and the cream-colored long skirt with cream fabric roses at the waist was first made as a one-of-a-kind for Mel Odom's personal collection by Tim Kennedy. Mel chose this gown to be duplicated for the UFDC since it so beautifully fit the convention theme of "Opulence and Elegance."

149

Secondary Prices for Gene Dolls & Costumes

An interesting phenomenon has arisen with the buying and selling of *Gene*. With many contemporary dolls, handling and undressing them is discouraged, but with *Gene* the reverse is true. As a result, collectors feel free to buy a dressed doll and then undress her and sell the dress, or to keep the dress and sell the doll. On e-Bay and other sources where *Gene* dolls can be found for sale, it is not unusual to find the different components sold individually. In this price list, however, we are referring to dressed dolls in excellent condition.

The category of one-of-a-kind *Gene* dolls is also not addressed in this price list. Some of the original designer outfits command high prices, as do the one-of-a-kinds which have been created for the *Gene* conventions and charity auctions, such as the FAO Las Vegas showgirls. However, because they must be considered on an individual basis, we are limiting our secondary prices to the Ashton-Drake dolls and costumes that are available to the general public.

The limited edition dolls and costumes and the early retired pieces have shown the most activity on the secondary market. Some of the recently retired pieces are still available from dealers and can still be found at their original retail price.

The following are some of the active dolls and costumes. Completed transactions of Internet sales during 1999 were tracked and the going prices at shows and dealer prices were also considered. Where prices differ substantially, the wider ranges indicate the disparity. Because fewer of the smaller limited editions have shown up on the market to be tracked the variations in prices are wider.

Name	Original Price	Value Now	Notes
A Night at Versailles	$90	$200 -$375	1997. 1st FAO LE:5,000
Afternoon Off	$29.95	$35-$50	1996. Retired 1998
Atlantic City Beauty	N/A	$1,200-$2,000	1996 Convention package
Broadway Medley	N/A	$305-$570	1998 Convention LE 900
Covent Garden	$99.99	$80-105	1998 NAILED Exclusive
Holiday Magic	$44.95	$300-$350+	1996. 1st Dealer LE 2,000
Midnight Gamble	$99.95	$105-$140	1998 LE 9,500
Midnight Romance	$89.95	$150-175	1997. 1st NAILED Exclusive
Monaco	$69.95	$85-$105	1995. Retired 1998
My Favorite Witch	N/A	$1,500-$1,850	1997 Convention LE 350
On the Avenue	$90	$135-$295	1998. LE 5,000
On the Set	N/A	$350-$425	1999. UFDC LE 350
Pin-up	$69.95	$75-$95	1996. Retired 1999
Premiere	$69.95	$500-$850	1995. Retired 1996
Ransom in Red	$44.95	$50-$75	1998. LE 7,500
Santa Fe Celebration	N/A	$350-$400	1999 LE 250
The King's Daughter	$99.95	$200-$300	1997. LE 5,000
Warmest Wishes	$110	$110-$140	1997. FAO

Retired Dolls and Costumes that can still be found at original list price:

Afternoon Off	$29.95 and up	Mondarin Mood	$34.95
Blond Lace	$29.95	Pink Lightning	$29.95
Blue Evening	$29.95	Promenade	$29.95
Crème De Cassis	$79.95 and up	Sea Spree	$34.95
Crimson Sun	$29.95	Striking Gold	$29.95
Iced Coffee	$79.95 and up	White Hyancinth	$79.95 and up

Index

About the Author

Carolyn Cook has long been active in the doll world. For over ten years she was associated with *Doll Reader* magazine, ending as Editor/Publisher. She has written numerous articles about dolls for publications such as *Contemporary Doll Collector, Doll News,* and *The Joy of Collecting,* was co-author of the book *I Had That Doll!* and acted as editor/contributor for several books for the United Federation of Doll Clubs, including *A French Tapestry* for the 1998 national convention. In 1997 she introduced a new publication to serious doll collectors, the *Doll Journal.* And, yes, she does collect *Gene* dolls!

THE GENE BOOK

SHE'D RATHER DANCE
IT'S A FROSTY TANGERINE ROMANCE
SEE PAGE 3

RETIREMENTS
WHAT'S NOT—IS HOT!
SEE PAGE 27 FOR INFO

MENU FOR ROMANCE
A FEAST FOR THE EYES—AND
EARS
See Page 2

WE'D LIKE TO SEND YOU A FREE GENE CATALOG

Mail us the Request Form below and we'll send you the Gene catalog starring the current collection of fabulous dolls, costumes and accessories. And be the first to catch all the latest "newsreels" on Miss Gene Marshall, including guest appearances by artist Mel Odom, special events and more!

To order from the current
Gene Marshall Collection
or to find a Gene retailer near you,
call our toll-free Gene Hotline
1-888-FOR-GENE
(1-888-367-4363)

Gene®

SHARE
THE DREAM

Get Your Free Copy of the Official Gene Marshall Catalog.

Fill out this postage-paid card and mail it to us
today, or call the Gene Hotline at
1-888-FOR-GENE/367-4363

Signature   Date

Name (please print clearly)

(   )
Telephone

Address   City   State   Zip

THE ASHTON-DRAKE GALLERIES • 9200 North Maryland Avenue, Niles, Illinois 60714-9853
V34424

THE REVIEWS ARE IN...

"A star is born, and she's a doll. Gene is really something else."
—Frank DeCaro
The New York Times

"Gene is the hottest doll in thirty years."
—Gary Ruddell, founding publisher, *Doll Reader Magazine* Contributing Editor, "Barbie Doll Collector's Handbook"

"Stock up on Gene Marshall dolls."
—*Cosmopolitan magazine*

"It's the stuff of Hollywood legends: an unknown young woman is discovered and becomes a star."
—*Santa Barbara News*

"A hauntingly flawless face, a spectacular wardrobe, and a seductive story line."
—Beauregard Houston-Montgomery, *Doll Reader magazine*

"All eyes are on Gene Marshall!"
—*The Chicago Sun-Times*

Gene®

Share the Dream